# 33 THINGS

## TO TALK TO KIDS

## ABOUT GLOBAL

## CHALLENGES

CONSTANZE NIEDERMAIER

33 Things to Talk to Kids about Global Challenges/Constanze Niedermaier — 1st ed.
First Printing: 2015

ISBN 978-0-9864131-1-7

Constanze Niedermaier/Whyzz LLC

www.whyzz.com


Ordering Information:
Special discounts are available on quantity purchases. For details, contact the publisher at the above listed address.
U.S. trade bookstores and wholesalers:
Please contact Whyzz LLC, CN@whyzz.com.

*"Kid, you'll move mountains!"* (Dr. Seuss)

To T & R.

# ABOUT THE AUTHOR

Constanze Niedermaier is the mother of two beautiful, curious kids and the founder and CEO of Whyzz. Whyzz is a media company that helps parents raise global citizens by equipping them with tools to explain the world to their children. She started Whyzz when her first child was born and she realized that she was in need of creative tools to answer her little girl's questions and raise a curious, open-minded child of the 21st century.

*Constanze Niedermaier*

# CONTENT

Introduction                                                    6
How to Use this Book                                            8

**Chapter 1. People**

5 quarters          —    Poverty                               12
Globe               —    Inequality                            15
Pajamas             —    Homelessness                          18
Peanut Butter       —    Malnutrition                          21
Birth Certificate   —    Identity                              24
Leash               —    Violence                              27
Water Bottle        —    Terrorism                             30
Tent                —    Refugees                              33
Shopping Cart       —    Food Waste                            36
Hair Brush          —    Water Access                          39
Toilet Brush        —    Sanitation                            42
Graduation Hat      —    Gender Equality                       45
Wedding Cake        —    Child Marriage                        48
Chocolate           —    Child Labor                           51
Passport            —    Modern Day Slavery                    54
Tire Tube           —    Education                             57
Elevator Buttons    —    Urbanization                          60
Lock                —    Cyber Security                        63
Sugar Cube          —    Diseases                              66

# CONTENT

Healthcare — Bicycle 69
Soap — Superbugs 72

## Chapter 2. Planet
Kayak — Melting Ice Caps 76
Flashlight — Severe Weather 79
Pearls — Ocean Acidification 82
Sweater — Energy Crisis **85**
Plastic Bag — Overconsumption 88
Rubber Boots — Overfishing **91**
Balloon — Endangered Animals 94
Origami — Deforestation 97
Cook Pot — Energy Poverty **100**
No Idling Sign — Air Pollution **103**
Flyswatter — Sustainable Agriculture 106

## Chapter 3. One Earth
Ship — All in One Boat 110

Sustainable Development Goals 112
Stories of Hope 115
Glossary 117
Sources 120

# INTRODUCTION

When I see the enthusiasm shown by children as young as five in changing the world for the better by recycling or collecting money for charity, I ponder at what age parents should start explaining global issues and challenges to their kids. Should we keep silent about climate change, inequality, poverty, food insecurity, water shortage, or child labor until middle school or introduce those issues as soon as they might understand the topic?

Empowerment and reassurance are two very important concepts in raising children. We want to empower our children to stand up for themselves, believe in their abilities, and make their own decisions. And we want to reassure them about a safe and happy life. I believe that a non-frightening explanation of what poverty means all around the world, or the impacts of climate change, together with ideas about how to make a difference, is empowering and reassuring to our kids because we take them seriously and show them how to help.

The world changes at a tremendous pace, and a challenge faced by some of us is going to affect each one of us. Children should learn about ways to end, reduce or mitigate the world's biggest challenges like poverty, injustice and climate change as early as they can process the information. They are the

# INTRODUCTION

future consumers, leaders, decision makers, and inheritors of the earth.

With this book I would like to help parents talk about issues that current and future generations will be facing, and goals for a brighter future for all humans. No child is too young to make a difference! Why not give them that confidence early on? We owe it to our children to raise them to become global citizens who are aware of the interrelations between everything that is happening in the world.

2015 is an important year for people and our planet. The Climate Change Summit and the United Nations release of the 2015 *Sustainable Development Goals,* also called the *Global Goals*, will get world leaders to commit to a better and more sustainable world. Based on those goals, it depends on every human being — young and old, rich and poor — to help save the world.

Use the "things" presented in this book to start conversations about a world in which each child can go to school, receive health care, protection, and food security, and live on a healthy planet with rich biodiversity. I am hoping this book leads to many meaningful conversations in your family that will help you make a difference together.

# HOW TO USE THIS BOOK

"33 Things to Talk to Kids about Global Challenges" is meant to help you as parents to have conversations with your kids about what is going on in the world.

I've designed the book so that you can take advantage of the topics presented in one of two ways. You can read the stories in advance, and then discuss each topic with your children in your own words. Or you can read the articles aloud to your kids and discuss them afterwards. Or perhaps you'll choose to do both, depending on the nature of or setting for the discussion.

Each article uses an everyday object as the "hook" to start the conversation. At the end of each article, there is a graphic that shows how all topics are directly or indirectly connected to one another. The last paragraph of each topic gives your children some ideas for how everyone can make a difference in the world.

Read about the U.N.'s Sustainable Development Goals, also called the Global Goals at the end of the book and find the matching

# HOW TO USE THIS BOOK

Global Goal next to each article. Stories of Hope show your children that change is possible.

A word that is written in Italic font is explained in the glossary, a word that has a little * is the subject of an article.

For all the topics of this book it is important to:
1) Talk to your children in an age-appropriate, truthful way. You know best how much your children can handle. Some facts that might be disturbing for young children are not mentioned in this book. It is up to you to include more details or leave out others, depending on your child's age and previous knowledge.
2) Empower your kids to help save the planet. No child is too young to make a difference.

There is no need to follow the order presented in the book — just pick a "thing" and discover its story. If a "why" question is raised by your child when discussing a particular subject, search the www.whyzz.com database you may find the answer there.

# CHAPTER 1
# PEOPLE

# POVERTY

Think about what you can buy for $1.25. A can of soda, two bananas, or a candy bar? Now imagine $1.25 is all you have to live on for an entire day — for food, clothing, school supplies, medicine, and housing. Every single day of the year. $1.25. Five Quarters.

Over one billion — that is one in seven — people live in extreme poverty, most in *developing countries* but also in wealthy nations in the developed world. That means the amount of money they can spend per day equals the amount of $1.25 in the U.S. Poverty has many levels; extreme poverty is the worst. Someone who is able to pay rent for an apartment but can't afford food is considered poor; likewise someone who has food but no clean water, or no money for education or medical services. People who live in poverty are very unlikely to fulfill their potential or live healthy and happy lives.

Poverty is especially dramatic for children: half of all children in the world live in poverty. If children don't have enough to eat they often get very sick, they don't grow properly and their brains don't develop the way they should. Many poor kids can't go to school so that their chances of getting out of poverty are very slim.

There is no easy answer to the question of why so many people live in poverty. An individual might be poor because of illness or

# POVERTY

the death of a close relative. They may have lost their job or had to flee a natural disaster or war.

In communities or whole countries, poverty is largely due to inequality* — it is a matter of who owns land, farm animals, oil, wood, factories, or knowledge and who doesn't. The gap between those who have and those who don't is growing increasingly larger; today already a few people own the majority of the world's wealth.

There also is no single solution to fight global poverty. However if all children grow up healthy and well nourished, and if they receive a decent education*, chances increase that they will be able to escape poverty. If there were enough nutritious food, healthcare* and schools for everyone, experts believe that extreme poverty could be eradicated by the year 2030.

**What you can do**

Get educated about global poverty and try to understand the many reasons for poverty. Donate time, money, and goods to organizations that help poor people.

## Cause and Effect

When you read the articles in this book, think about the relationship between a topic and poverty: ask yourself whether the topic is a cause or an effect of poverty. You will come to understand that poverty is one of the two most urgent issues for the world to solve. Do you know which one is the other one?

# CONNECT SOME DOTS

# INEQUALITY

How about a game: Close your eyes and spin a globe. Now stop the rotation with putting your finger on any country — still with your eyes closed. (You could also use a world map on the computer). Now imagine what your life would be like if you were born in that country. Would you have a big family? What foods would you eat? Would you go to school or work? Would you have a nice home and many toys? Would you be able to go to college and find a decent job after you've graduated?

Your chances of leading a happy, healthy and successful life are very much determined by where you were born and where you grow up. Different countries have different cultures, as well as different opportunities for children to be strong, healthy, and well educated. Many countries in the world are extremely poor; they have few schools, not enough doctors, and a scarcity of food. They can't provide safety for their citizens due to war or lawlessness. In many countries women don't have the right to choose how they want to live their lives, or to have a job. People with disabilities have an even harder life.

Inequality is the term to describe a situation in which people don't have the same opportunities. Inequality means that if you live in the "wrong" place in the world it is very hard or even impossible for you to become the grown-up you wish to become. Your disadvantages start the day you are born. Your body and brain

# INEQUALITY

can't develop properly if you don't have enough food. Chances are that you will have to work, you can't go to school or you will drop out before high school. Even if you finish school, there might not be any jobs for you to make a living.

To compare: a child that is born into a family that has enough money and lives in a safe environment will have nutritious food, see doctors regularly, have books and toys, can go to school and college, will do sports and travel. His or her chances of leading a happy life are significantly higher.

Inequality doesn't only exist between countries, but also within the same country, even in the same city. If you were born on the wrong side of town in a low-income neighborhood, your chances of succeeding are much smaller than those of a person growing up in a wealthy neighborhood.

## Social Mobility

What do you think? When people born in a disadvantaged place in the world want to leave to seek a better life, will they have a chance to do so? Do you think they will be able to fulfill their potential? Does that explain that only three percent of all 7 billion people worldwide migrate to a different country each year?

# CONNECT SOME DOTS

# HOMELESSNESS

There is a saying: "A house is made of walls and beams, a home is built of love and dreams." Does that mean that if you don't have a house to live in you can still have a home as long as there is love and dreams? Or does it mean that only if there is love and dreams in a house is it truly a home? What if there is neither a house nor love and dreams?

All over the world — in rich and poor countries alike — about 100 million people are homeless, many of them women and children. Homelessness means people don't have a safe place to sleep. They don't have a place to keep their belongings, spend time with their families, or feel protected. Often homelessness means people lose touch with family members, friends, or their community; when this happens, dreams of a better life start to fade.

For children, being homeless means there is no cozy bed to be tucked into by their parents. Often it means not even owning their own pajamas. They must sleep in shelters, cars, parks, or empty buildings — sometimes at a different place each night.

It also means they don't get to learn as much as other children, because they don't regularly attend school, or can't do their homework. They may get sick often, and they can't invite friends

# HOMELESSNESS

Global Goal
## #1

*No
Poverty*

for playdates. Their parents — if they are around at all — are often desperate about their own lives and unable to provide their children with the love and care they need. Homelessness is the biggest threat to a human's dignity.

The reasons people are homeless are mostly related to poverty*. Many homeless people can't find a job or don't earn enough money to pay for a home. Illness or disabilities may play a role; other times people are displaced by wars or natural disasters.

Escaping homelessness is very difficult without help from others. Governments and organizations provide solutions such as affordable housing, longterm shelters, education* programs, career training, and job opportunities. Equally important is what each of us can do: treat homeless people with the same respect as we treat everyone else.

## Shower buses and PJ drives

People who want to help are launching innovative projects to ease the burden of homelessness. Two examples are old public buses that are remolded into mobile showers, and charity drives to donate pajamas to homeless children.

## What you can do

Donate money, food, toys, school supplies, or clothes to homeless shelters in your community. Treat every person with the same respect with which you'd like to be treated.

# CONNECT SOME DOTS

# MALNUTRITION

Peanut butter might be a staple on your breakfast table. PBJ's are in fact very popular in the United States. A study once found that the average American will have eaten one thousand, five hundred peanut-butter sandwiches before finishing high school.[1]

Peanut butter isn't loved by all. Some people are allergic to peanuts and develop severe reactions when coming in contact with them. But for millions of people, especially children, a special form of peanut butter that contains added nutrients is actually a life saver. It is used as a therapeutic food, food that can heal from malnourishment.

Malnourishment means that a human body for a long time didn't get the vitamins and minerals it needs to be healthy. For children under the age of five this is particularly devastating because they won't grow properly, their brains won't develop as they should, and they become sick and often die. In many places around the world, especially in parts of Asia and of Africa, families are so poor that they can't afford nutritious food. Their village may have been hit by drought or flood that destroyed their harvests, their country may have been ravaged by war, or their farmland may have been used for crops like coffee or chocolate or cotton instead of planting grains, fruits and vegetables.

One in nine people in the world — mostly in *developing countries* — doesn't get enough to eat or enough nutrients to be healthy. For

# MALNUTRITION

many people, rice is their only regular meal; while this may stave off hunger, it lacks the protein, vitamins, and minerals necessary to stay healthy.

When children aren't well nourished they are too weak to play, or too hungry to learn in school. Yet hunger and malnutrition can be overcome. There is actually enough food on our planet for everyone. If individuals, companies, organizations and governments work together they can ensure that every human has sustainable access to nourishing food. Education, lending money to small farmers — especially to women and indigenous people — equal distribution of food and protecting ecosystems and biodiversity are solutions to end hunger and malnutrition* for good.

## Obesity

Malnutrition can also happen if people overeat. An increasing number of people eat too much, or too much that lacks nutritional value. Over time these people may become obese and develop severe illnesses like heart issues, diabetes, or cancer. There are about as many people in the world obese as there are those that don't have enough to eat. Isn't it strange that two very different sides of nutritional problems exist?

## What you can do

You can help by supporting local farmers in your area through buying their products. Make sure you often eat natural and healthy foods and never waste any food.

# CONNECT SOME DOTS

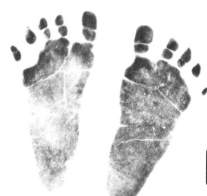

# IDENTITY

When you were born, the nurse or midwife most likely took prints of your feet. This was not a courtesy to your parents so they could keep a memento of how little you once were. It was a way to register you. Footprints are like fingerprints: no two are alike, which means that you can be identified by those prints. The footprints taken after birth become part of your birth certificate, along with your first and last name, date and time of birth, your gender, the city in which you were born, and the country of which you are a *citizen*. It also shows the name of your mother and generally your father.

Although a birth certificate is a person's most important document, almost 230 million children under the age of five have not had their births registered. That means one in three children don't officially exist! Many people think a birth certificate is just a formal document with little value. The truth is that without being officially registered, a person has no legal rights. Those include family rights like inheriting from relatives, the right to a last name, belonging to a family, or even getting married as grown-up. They also include citizen rights such as nationality, getting a passport, the right to go to school or receive basic health care*. Worst of all, not being registered and not being able to prove one's age denies humans the right to be protected from crime, violence* and *abuse*.

# IDENTITY

There are different reasons why so many children don't get registered. One is poverty* — such as when a mother can't afford health care and gives birth at home with no doctor or nurse present. Another reason is location — some families live in remote areas and a trip to the nearest government office is too far away. Some families are refugees* and are unable to live in the country of which they are citizens. Other reasons include beliefs, customs, laws or the lack of a functioning government system in place.

The right to be registered is a fundamental right. It is included in the *United Nations* Convention of the Rights of every Child, and it is the foundation upon which all other Human Rights are to be granted.

## Individuality

Besides your name, gender, age, and family, your identity is also defined by your beliefs, experiences, knowledge, friends, how you feel about yourself, the place you live, and your differences from other people. Identity means who you are. Every human has a unique identity and is special in his or her own way. Remember what Dr. Seuss says: "Today you are you, that is truer than true. There is no one that is youer than you."

**What you can do**

Don't take your rights as a citizen of your country for granted. Be aware of what it means to live in a society that protects its members.

# CONNECT SOME DOTS

# VIOLENCE

Some animals have an incredible sense of smell. For example, black bears can smell food eighteen miles away. Dogs are used to search for drugs at airports. Pigs can detect delicious truffles under trees. Perhaps most amazing of all, rats are used to find explosives! In Africa, huge rats that grow up to three feet long are walked on leashes to help people find landmines that can then be disarmed.

Landmines are explosives that were buried in the ground during a war to destroy "enemy" vehicles or people that passed over them. Even after a war is over they pose a great threat to people if they are not found.

Wars are just one form of violence; others include terrorism*, violent crime, or violence at home from parents to children or from spouse to spouse. Each year, hundreds of millions of children experience some form of violence. They see *atrocities* during a war, witness *abuse* at home, or are hit by their parents as a form of discipline. "All forms of violence against children, however light, are unacceptable."[1] Children have a right to grow up in safety and with peace of mind. Violence robs children of a chance to become healthy and happy adults.

The reasons for violence are often based on inequality*. People who can't find a job and make a decent living, or who didn't get a proper education can feel left out by society and turn their

# VIOLENCE

aggression towards others. Experts also blame some video games for why individuals become violent. And some experts say that violence spreads like a contagious disease* from one member of a community to another.

However, despite the many terrible things happening in the world, violence has actually decreased over the past few hundred years. People are generally better educated than in the past and education* is a proven way to reduce violence — it teaches ways to resolve conflicts. It increases patience, resilience, confidence, moral values*, and a sense of belonging to society. If everyone had the chance to go to school and have a decent job as a result, violence could be further reduced. Although there are many different reasons why people are violent to others, including them in a community and offering them hope for a better future goes a long way.

## Bullying

Bullying is a form of violence that is all too present in children's lives. Almost eighty percent of children say they have been bullied with words, physical violence, or online.

**What you can do**

You are responsible for yourself and your body! Always talk to a safe adult if anyone is hurting or threatening you. Stand up for kids that are bullied, make new friends, and practice kindness every day. Learn about different cultures so you can better understand other people.

# CONNECT SOME DOTS

# TERRORISM

Do you know why you need to empty your water bottle before going on an airplane? Liquids can contain explosives which makes a water bottle look like a potential weapon. There are strict rules for airplane travel since the time of the most spectacular act of terrorism the world has ever seen: The airplane attack on the World Trade Center in New York City in 2001.

All over the world people die or are severely wounded by terrorist attacks. Many people live in fear that their house or family could become a target because they might be at the wrong place at the wrong time. Terrorism means violence* against innocent people committed by individuals who seek attention for their cause. They might want to change a government or the way they are treated. Or they might not like groups of people that live in their country. Or they might want to fight for animal rights or against companies that damage the environment. In many cases, though, hatred is their main motivation for committing terrorist acts.

Terrorism exists all over the world. Terrorists come from different countries, have different backgrounds, different religious beliefs, and different reasons for their violent acts. Some commit their acts of terror in their home country and some abroad. What most of them have in common, though, is being affected by the inequalities* in the world. Individuals who feel excluded from their communities or feel they have no hope for a better life sometimes

# TERRORISM

follow ideas and leaders that tell them to hurt or kill other people, or to destroy buildings or pieces of art. With terror they think they can work for a cause they believe in. They don't care that their victims almost always are not directly responsible for the injustice they experience in life.

Terror causes much anxiety because nobody knows when a terrorist attack might happen. It also causes a lot of prejudice against people who look different or have a different faith. If a few people of a certain background or nationality commit a terrorist act, some people may assume that all people of that background are potential terrorists too.

There may not be an easy solution to end all terrorism. However, ending the harsh inequalities that exist everywhere in the world will provide the basis for less violence. Including everyone in our community is something all of us can do.

## Homegrown Terrorism

Also called domestic terrorism, means terror that citizens of a state commit against their fellow people. Examples are: the Oklahoma City bombing in 1995 that destroyed more than 300 buildings and killed 168 people or the shooting of nine black church goers in Charleston in 2015.

## What you can do

Treat all people with respect. A person isn't likely to become a terrorist just because he shares some common traits like home country, skin color, or religious belief with people who have committed a terrorist act. Very few people believe in violence against innocent people, but all people deserve to be treated with dignity.

# CONNECT SOME DOTS

# REFUGEES

Do you know how many people live in your town? Is the number more or less than 400,000? That is the number of refugees that live in tents and other temporary structures in the world's largest refugee camp in Kenya.

A refugee camp is a temporary settlement where refugees can stay for a short time before they find a new place to live. They are mostly built with tents and other quick-to-set-up shelters.

Many people in the world flee their homes and countries and become refugees because their life or freedom is endangered by war, or due to their religious beliefs, their political opinion, or their race. Other reasons to seek refuge are natural disasters or *epidemics*.

It is estimated that about fifty million people are living as refugees. Many must leave their homes very quickly and aren't able to pack any belongings. Many travel in extremely dangerous circumstances — in overcrowded boats, or by walking across deserts or over mountains without enough food or water. Not all who attempt such journeys survive. Especially children and older people are at great risk during their journeys.

Once refugees make it to a camp their ordeal isn't over. Numerous camps in crisis areas are overcrowded and poorly equipped to

# REFUGEES

serve large numbers of people. Poor sanitation*, lack of food and clean water*, and infectious diseases* make living conditions unsafe. But for families with nowhere else to go, a camp may become home for several years. Refugee children often don't get the chance to go to school, they may become severely ill or suffer *trauma* from the terrible experiences they've made. If they were born at the camp they might not even have a birth certificate* or *citizenship*.

Although it is every human's responsibility to help those in need, countries that are neighbors to crisis areas often struggle to deal with the large numbers of refugees. Governments all over the world therefore need to help solve the global refugee crises, even if they are far away from the affected country. Help includes money, food, shelter, and clothes — as well as allowing refugees to move to a different place in the world, become citizens of that country and start a new life.

## Bright kids

It is estimated that half of all refugees are younger than eighteen years old. Many of them are very bright but don't have a chance to go to school or college unless organizations or individuals work hard to bring education opportunities to these kids and offer scholarships for college degrees.

## What you can do

Donate clothes, computers, or phones to organizations that support refugees. Volunteer with a local organization to play with refugee children or to help them learn your language. Most important of all, lend a helping hand, give a smile and the feeling of being welcomed to people that are new to your country.

# CONNECT SOME DOTS

# FOOD WASTE

How often have you heard your parents tell you: "Finish your plate, in other countries children don't have any food at all"? But often you might have just put too much on that plate, or ordered too much in a restaurant, or your family filled up the shopping cart in the grocery store with more food than you could ever eat in a certain amount of time. Eventually, this food will end up in the garbage.

All over the world about one third of all foods are wasted — in every step from farm to fork. Did you know, for example that producing the meat for just half a burger requires as much water as taking a one-hour shower? The reason is that a cow needs enormous amounts of water to be raised, and it eats a lot of grains that could otherwise feed dozens of people. That means we are wasting water and grains for meat before we even get to "waste" food by not finishing what's on our plates.

Food is wasted during production, when farmers lack the latest knowledge to properly grow their crops or when severe weather destroys the harvest. It is wasted during transportation, when food goes bad due to the long distances it must travel to get to markets. It is wasted in the store, when it isn't sold before its expiration date. And it is wasted in peoples' homes, when food that is no longer needed is thrown in the trash can and added to our *landfills*.

# FOOD WASTE

If there wasn't any food waste and all the food that is currently produced in the world would actually be eaten — there would be no hunger in the world. But food waste is not only a major problem for those that don't get access to food, it also has a significant impact on our environment. If no food was wasted, forests would remain valuable *ecosystems* and not be cut down for more agriculture, oceans would retain their rich biodiversity if fishing were kept at sustainable levels, groundwater would remain clear of pesticides and fertilizer, and our atmosphere would contain fewer dangerous greenhouse gases.

Finishing up your plate every day won't solve the problem. But thinking about what kind of food and especially how much of it we need to be healthy and strong goes a long way. What we put in our grocery cart has a big impact on our world.

## Thrown in the garbage...

On average, every person in the United States throws away two hundred pounds of food each year — enough to fill a 90,000 seat football stadium every day.[1]

## What you can do

Think about what you eat! Eat meat and seafood in moderation, buy local and seasonal products, and don't waste your food! Before buying or ordering food — think about how much you will actually finish eating.

# CONNECT SOME DOTS

# WATER ACCESS

There is a saying: "Pretty hair needs good care". Many children in some African countries wear their hair extremely short because the water available for bathing is often less than one cup. That is far too little to wash long hair. Often there is not even enough water for drinking and cooking.

For most of us, getting a glass of water or taking a shower is as easy as turning on the faucet. For millions of people in *developing countries,* getting water is a matter of survival that dictates everything they do.

Women and girls in these countries walk many hours every day to find a well or a water truck so they can bring heavy loads of water home to their families. There isn't any time left to go to school or earn money in a job. Often the water isn't clean for drinking, which means people get really sick. And to grow crops or raise animals for food, water is far too limited.

Water is life — for humans, animals and plants. Less than three percent of Earth's water is freshwater; the rest is salty ocean water. Yet the problem isn't so much the amount of fresh water, but the lack of access to it.

Agriculture and production of goods use a lot of the water that could otherwise be used for drinking. Did you know that a single

# WATER ACCESS

large bottle of milk requires one thousand bottles of water to produce? And that one pair of jeans requires eleven thousand bottles? Because so many people in the *developed world* pay a lot of money for these goods, water is used to produce them. Another reason for the lack of clean water is that so many people don't have a toilet* with a sewage system, so human waste contaminates groundwater or lakes. Or droughts may dry up freshwater sources.

Solutions to bring water to every human include rolling water containers to make the transport easier, water purification systems, and well drilling. Remarkable success has already been achieved over the past twenty years. However, about 750 million people still need *sustainable* solutions.

## Water Cycle

There isn't any new water coming to Earth. All the water that is here has been here for millions of years. And even though all the water we use goes back into the water cycle, chances are it won't be available to humans as freshwater. We need to acknowledge that water is a very precious resource that we should not take for granted.

# CONNECT SOME DOTS

# SANITATION

True or false: More people have access to a mobile phone than a toilet. Well, hard to believe but it is actually true, about 2.6 billion people in the world are not able to use a clean and safe toilet. Only around one billion don't have access to a mobile phone. In western civilizations the biggest concern is how to keep toilets clean — the fact that there is the luxury of a toilet everywhere is taken for granted.

In many rural areas of China and India in particular, people do their business outside. This is called open defecation. Half the population of the huge country of India doesn't have access to a bathroom.

The main reason for the lack of proper sanitation is poverty*. A working toilet not only requires a bowl to sit on, but an entire, expensive waste system. Other reasons toilets don't exist in many areas are lack of water for proper flushing, and local beliefs and traditions. In some villages people meet for public squatting as a social event. In others, people are superstitious — they believe that digging holes and building toilets will bring bad luck. Some just don't see the necessity of using a toilet.

But open defecation is a huge health hazard. It causes death for millions, prevents children from going to school, and threatens the environment. It can also hurt peoples' dignity. That's why toilets

# SANITATION

can change the world! When human waste is handled safely in sewage systems, water for drinking and cooking is no longer at risk of contamination. Dangerous germs are kept from being ingested by humans. Malnutrition*, blindness, and life-threatening illnesses are prevented.

When there are private toilets, girls can stay in school and learn, they won't face violence* in hidden areas or they won't get sick by not being able to empty their bodies.

All over the world there are countless projects to bring toilets to every community. These projects require money, as well as creativity in finding feasible solutions for different regions. They also require efforts to educate and convince community leaders, employers, and individuals of the benefits and urgency of clean toilets.

**What you can do**

Look for innovation labs and science fairs at your school to join the Reinvent the Toilet Challenge.[1]

## Toilet Facts[2]

- The average person spends three years of his or her life sitting on the toilet.
- Before unused food ends up in the toilet it must travel thirty feet through your intestines.
- Names for toilets: loo, dunny, bog, khazi, privy, latrine, place of easement, house of honor.

# CONNECT SOME DOTS

# GENDER EQUALITY

Do you agree with the following statements? Girls wear pink, they are nice and kind, they cooperate, and they don't need to go to college because they will get married and have babies. Boys on the other hand like sports, they are competitive, they don't do household chores, and they might lead a company or government one day.

Those statements are called gender stereotypes. A stereotype is a general belief about an entire group of people. Stereotypes can be positive or negative, but since they are so general — "all girls" or "all boys" — they hardly ever give any accurate information about an individual person.

The reason stereotypes, are bad is that they force people into roles or behaviors that they might not identify with. If everyone thinks that running a household is a woman's task, then women are more likely to be forced into that role by society, even though she might think cooking is the most boring thing ever. Being forced into roles simply because society deems them appropriate means people aren't treated with respect for being unique with special talents and interests.

All over the world, gender stereotypes — and the traditions and beliefs that were formed through these stereotypes — lead to severe inequalities for women. Two thirds of women worldwide cannot read. Many women cannot buy land for agriculture or

# GENDER EQUALITY

housing. They can't get credit from a bank to start a business, or go to school, or visit a doctor. They are trapped in a never-ending cycle of poverty*. In many countries it is okay if a husband hits his wife or doesn't allow her to leave the house. When working outside the house women are paid less money than men for doing the same job — or they are not hired for a position simply because they are a woman. Relatively few large companies are run by women. Governments, too, have mostly men in decision-making positions.

However, when girls are allowed to go to school, and eventually to college, their whole community is better off. Healthy and educated women have healthy and educated children. They contribute a great deal to the well-being of their country. Seventy-seven countries have a female president or head of state. Women can achieve anything when equal rights make it possible!

## Suffragettes

Women in the United States and the United Kingdom were only granted the right to vote about a hundred years ago. Another term for the right to vote is suffrage; that's why the women who stood up for their rights were called Suffragettes.

# CONNECT SOME DOTS

# CHILD MARRIAGE

In our culture a wedding is a joyful occasion to celebrate the fact that two adults have fallen in love and have decided to spend their lives together. Often there will be a cake and music and dancing for all the guests but especially the newlyweds to enjoy.

For fifteen million girls each year, marriage is not a reason to celebrate. They aren't excited about wearing a fancy dress or about beautiful flower decorations. Child marriage happens in every region in the world and in families of all different religions. In *developing countries* such as Bangladesh, India, and Nigeria, one in three girls is forced to wed before her eighteenth birthday — sometimes as young as eight years old.

In some countries it's a tradition that parents arrange the marriage of their young daughters. In other countries, girls are simply valued less than boys; giving them as brides to much older men ensures them a place in society. And very often, poverty* is the reason girls are married, even though they are still children and don't have a say in their marriage.

Becoming a child bride has dire effects on a girl's life. She is forced to quit school and give up the chance to get an education and make a decent living later in life. She most often will be forced to work very hard for her new family and will face violence

# CHILD MARRIAGE

if she doesn't obey. Her health is at great risk because being pregnant and giving birth is very dangerous for a young girl; many die in childbirth. And if the girl survives, her baby often won't live to its first birthday. A girl's poor community suffers from child marriage too. Not giving girls a chance to grow up strong and healthy, to get an education and work in jobs that support the family and the whole community makes it impossible for entire towns and even countries to overcome extreme poverty.

There is no easy solution to end child marriage. Enabling girls to go to school until they are eighteen years old by supporting their families is the most powerful tool to end child marriage. Another crucial step is convincing their communities that educated girls will allow them to give back to society by earning money and raising healthy and educated children. Better lives for girls mean better lives for boys — and for everyone in the community.[1]

## What you can do

Raise awareness for the issue of girls in developing countries by talking to your friends about it. Ask your teachers to discuss the issue in school.

## The Girl Effect

Girls can change the world. Ask your parents to watch a video with you on the Internet called "The Girl Effect" to understand why girls can have a strong impact in solving the world's challenges. To learn more about how to give girls a chance in life visit the website GirlsNotBrides.org

# CONNECT SOME DOTS

# CHILD LABOR

"Chocolate is ground from the beans of happiness,"[1] someone once said. Most people would agree that eating chocolate makes them feel happy. Is that true for you too?

Chocolate is made from cocoa beans, most of which are grown in West Africa. The workers who harvest the beans are often children. Other ingredients of chocolate, including sugar, palm oil, and nuts also often utilize child labor for their harvests. These children work twelve to sixteen exhausting hours in the fields every day, sometimes even without any pay. For them, chocolate really doesn't mean happiness.

About eleven percent of all children between five and seventeen years of age worldwide have to work. As a result, they don't receive any education, don't have time to play and their health is often at great risk due to dangerous working conditions and long working hours that young bodies are not made to endure.

Many experts say that the situation for these children would be even worse if they didn't have a chance to go to work and earn money for their very poor families. They argue that while child labor should not be prohibited, in general, there must be laws that guarantee children's safety, decent payment, and time to rest and learn.

# CHILD LABOR

Child labor is mostly a result of extreme poverty* and inequality* throughout the world. When all parents were able to earn enough money to support their families, their children can attend school instead of working in a factory or field. Yet the growing demand in developed countries for cheaper products, combined with the profit goals of large companies, make working conditions for many people in the *developing world* more dangerous and lower paid.

Products that are made under terrible working conditions range from toys and electronics to food and cosmetics to clothes and furniture — the list is endless. To improve the situation, governments and corporations need to change the way workers are treated, and they need to support those who aren't able to work. In the meantime, each of us can make informed decisions about what and how much we buy.

## Chimney Sweeps, Gillie Boys & Powder Monkeys

Before child labor was forbidden by law in western countries kids would work very hard: for example, as Chimney Sweeps, who crawled up and cleaned chimneys; as Gillie Boys, who prepared bait and hooks for fisherman; or as Powder Monkeys, who carried gun powder for cannons on warships and in forts.

## What you can do

Buy from brands that treat their workers well. Discuss with your parents if the price that shops ask for a product might be too low to pay workers a decent salary. Help spread the word about how many people in the world must struggle to make a living.

# CONNECT SOME DOTS

# MODERN DAY SLAVERY

Did you know that there are more slaves in the world today than at any time in history[1]? You've probably studied the topic of slavery in the United States in the 18th and 19th centuries, and the *abolitionist movement* to end it. However, slavery did not end in the 19th century. Around 30 million people worldwide are sold and forced to work for no pay — often threatened with violence against themselves or their families if they don't comply.

While three countries — India, China, and Pakistan — account for over half of the world's slaves, modern-day slavery exists in every country in the world, including the United States.

There are many ways a person might end up being trafficked (another word for being enslaved and sold). Extreme poverty* is often a factor. The hope for a better life in another country, or the false promise of a legitimate job may lure unsuspecting victims to a trafficker. They may then be kidnapped and told that they must work to repay the costs of bringing them to the new place, only for that time period to be extended indefinitely. They may have their passport taken away by their trafficker, or have no passport to begin with, which limits their options for escape. They may be physically abused, or be threatened with violence* against their family if they don't work hard enough or try to flee. Victims may be men, women, or — all too often — children or teens. In any case, slavery means terrible suffering for its victims.

# MODERN DAY SLAVERY

There are many types of jobs in which forced labor occurs frequently. Garment manufacturing, hotels, restaurants, nightclubs, construction, mining, nail salons, agriculture, fishing, and domestic household work are some examples. Escaping slavery is nearly impossible unless there are people or organizations willing to help. Ending slavery is a goal every government in the world must pursue — not simply because freedom is a fundamental human right, but because people who live in freedom and work in well-paid jobs contribute to the greater good of their communities.

## Chains and foot shackles?

In the 21ˢᵗ century, victims of slavery may not be immediately recognizable. Unlike the kinds of slavery you may have read about in books, modern-day slaves don't wear chains or foot shackles. Yet they are still controlled by intimidation and violence*, and trapped by the very real bonds of slavery.

## What you can do

Get informed about modern-day slavery and educate your friends about it. Speak to a trusted adult if you suspect somebody you meet might be kept in slavery.

# CONNECT SOME DOTS

# EDUCATION

For some kids, getting to school is uncomfortable; for others it is outright dangerous. In some parts of the world children must cross dangerous rivers in tire tubes. In others, kids balance atop broken suspension bridges, on unsecured ladders or narrow mountain paths. Some ride on bulls, on top of boats, or in horse carriages to get to school. These trips often take hours every day.

Despite the hardships many are willing to endure in order to get even a basic education, 59 million children worldwide can't go to school at all. An additional 120 million children attend school for a short time but don't complete sixth grade. One in four young children in the developing world are unable to read a sentence.

There are several reasons so many children can't go to school. Their parents may be too poor to pay for school supplies, or they may need their children to work and support the family. In some cases the family may have had to flee their home because of war or disaster. If the child is a girl, she may have been raised in a culture in which girls are not allowed to get an education. Finally, many communities simply don't have a school or teachers.

In the developed world, too, many children are at a big disadvantage and do much worse in school than their peers — just because their

# EDUCATION

family lives in poverty. They are sent to schools that don't have enough money, and their parents are unable to help them with their homework.

When children don't attend school, their opportunities for leading a happy and healthy life are slim. Their chances of finding a well-paying job are very small. Their health is at risk because they lack the information to help them prevent or fight diseases*. They won't learn about their rights as a citizen of a country. A life of missed education means a life of missed opportunities.

However, if girls and boys are able to finish school, they have a chance to fulfill their potential, to escape poverty*, to raise healthy and educated children, and to give back to their community in many ways. As Nelson Mandela said: *"Education is the most powerful weapon you can use to change the world."*

## What you can do

Learn as much as you can, in school and outside of school. Value every opportunity you get to learn.

## Khan Academy

Online learning tools like the Khan Academy may bring educational opportunities to children all over the world who aren't able to attend school, or in places where teachers don't have the skills to teach kids all they need to know.

# CONNECT SOME DOTS

Urbanization · Poverty · Cyber Security · Sustainable Agriculture · Identity · Education · Inequality · Malnutrition · Overfishing · Healthcare · Violence · Terrorism

# URBANIZATION

The world's fastest elevator will start transporting people to the 95 floors of a building in Guangzhou, China in 2016. It will reach a speed of 45 mph (or 72 km/h) and will get to the top floor in 43 seconds. The same building complex will hold a total of 94 elevators to bring workers to their offices.

The reason why super fast elevators are being developed is that ever growing numbers of people are moving into cities to work and to live in tall buildings. Already half of the world's population lives in cities, and experts believe the number will grow to more than two thirds by 2050. Moving from rural to urban areas brings opportunities. One's chances of finding work are much higher in a city. There are usually more and better schools and healthcare facilities than in the country. Clean water and sufficient food supplies are more common. And people need to travel much shorter distances to organize their lives.

However, migration from rural areas to cities often isn't a choice people make voluntarily. Often they are forced by poverty*, lack of clean water*, illness, or when their farm lands have been destroyed by *land degradation*.

Urbanization, which means mass migration of people from the country to the city, brings many challenges. When cities' populations grow too fast there isn't enough housing; there aren't enough

# URBANIZATION

jobs, or schools, or police, or hospitals. Waste water and garbage may create massive pollution. Animals' habitats may be destroyed to build more houses. Inequality* may become a big issue when very poor people live next to very rich families. Natural disasters pose a major threat for areas in which many people live close together. Diseases* can spread quickly. And more motor vehicles contribute to air pollution* and accidents.

In 2030 there will be 41 so-called megacities with more than 10 million inhabitants. China might soon count 130 million people (almost half of the population of the USA) in one city. Currently, Tokyo, Japan is the most populous city in the world with 37 million people — and it is also the safest. If managed well, all cities, even very big ones, can provide many opportunities for enriching people's lives.

## Slums

Slums are areas of big cities where very poor people live — often in shacks with no electricity or running water. In some cities in Africa and Asia, half the population of a city lives in slums. Shantytown, favela or barrio are other names for slums. Although slums are now more common in the developing world, they were common in European and North American cities until about a hundred years ago.

**What you can do**

If you live in a city, help keep it clean. Treat people and places in your city with respect. Be mindful of other people's needs because everyone lives so close together.

# CONNECT SOME DOTS

# CYBER SECURITY

Not too long ago, back in the days before personal computers and the Internet, people kept confidential information such as their bank account details, Social Security number, or health records locked away in their desks or special closets. Companies and government offices also had safe places to store confidential information that was printed on paper or recorded on audio or video files.

Today, over two billion people are connected to the Internet. We organize our whole lives on the web, from online banking to email, document sharing, social networking, and transferring our health records. The world is now reliant on the Internet for services like traffic control, warning systems, or government and military infrastructure.

Being connected through computer networks such as the Internet brings many opportunities. People have access to their information and documents wherever they are in the world, and it's easy to work together with someone in a different place. When machines are operated through connected computer networks, their efficiency and safety is highly increased.

However, *hyper-connectivity* also carries risks. Cyber-attacks and digital spying have become a bigger threat to a nation's security than the risk of terrorism*. To commit a cyber-crime, a computer is used in what is called "hacking" to steal someone's information or destroy

# CYBER SECURITY

information through a computer virus. It may entail stealing money by transferring it from one bank account to another, or taking on a person's identity (so called "identity theft") with the data like name, social security number and address that is found on a computer. You've heard of cyber bullying — using the Internet to harass or bully someone online — can also be a cyber crime.

Cyber crime is a major problem for governments and companies. Confidential data might fall into the hands of other governments or a company's competitors. Control systems can be disrupted, causing severe accidents. The whole world's financial systems could be attacked, potentially causing many people to lose money. Cyber crime can affect our lives in many ways that range from inconvenience to live threatening. Keeping computers, smart phones and other devices as well as all computer networks safe is a major challenge we all face.

## Internet of things

Experts believe that in the very near future many objects like refrigerators or television or washing machines, will be connected to the Internet and communicate with other objects. When machines directly connect with other machines, the risks of cyber crime gets even bigger.

## What you can do

Protect your computer with a hard-to-guess password, and never share your password with anyone. Keep private information confidential and never post it to social media sites. Don't click links in emails from unknown senders, and most importantly, never trust anyone you meet on the Internet.

# CONNECT SOME DOTS

# DISEASES

"A spoonful of sugar makes the medicine go down," sings Mary Poppins. Wouldn't it be nice if the doctor simply gave you a sugar cube instead of poking your arm with a needle when it's time for shots? Then kids would like immunizations instead of being afraid of them. There is actually one vaccination that is given with a spoonful of sugar: Polio, a disease that paralyses people and for which there is no cure, was almost entirely eradicated after hundreds of millions of children swallowed sugar with the vaccine liquid.

Having a disease means the body or parts of the body aren't working properly and doctors know a reason for this condition based on the symptoms a person shows. Some diseases are contagious — they may be transmitted through the air, through blood, or other bodily contact (for example, by touching something that is infected, then transferring the germs to your mouth). Other diseases are caused by the foods you eat or by your lifestyle, some you inherit from your family.

Most diseases can be cured, and many more can be prevented or lessened by choices you make. But not all people are lucky enough to be able to avoid or treat them. Even simple and low-cost prevention is often out of reach for people living in poverty*. Vaccinations, medicines, and preventive solutions like bed nets

# DISEASES

(which protect people from malaria spreading mosquitos) aren't accessible for poor people or those who live in remote areas.

Each minute, twenty-one children under the age of five die of diseases, most of them preventable. If only those children had vaccinations, vitamins, clean water* and other things that we take for granted, many of them could be saved.

In all of human history, only one disease has completely been eradicated — smallpox. However, scientists are optimistic that polio will be next, and that in the next fifteen years significant progress will be made in eradicating malaria, measles and other severe illnesses.

## Small Planet

In our connected world in which people, products, and news travel long distances in a very short time, diseases don't stay local either. Contagious diseases have the potential to become worldwide *epidemics* very quickly. Globalization has many benefits but also some downsides.

**What you can do**

Learn about health, nutrition, and the human body so that you can make healthy choices. Be grateful for the opportunity to have regular doctor's check-ups — even if it means an occasional shot!

# CONNECT SOME DOTS

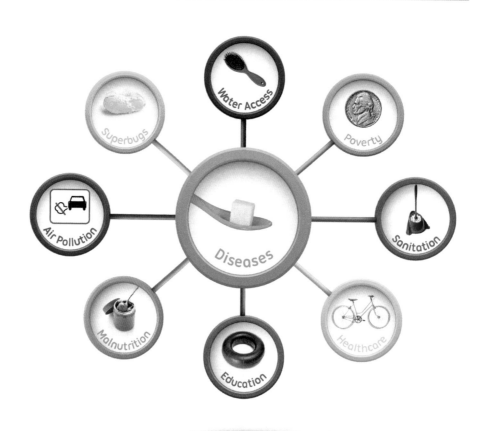

# HEALTHCARE

Riding a bike, like other forms of exercise, is good for your health; it helps develop your leg muscles, your heart, and your lungs. Can you think of other ways a bicycle might support health?

In many countries, people live far away from doctors and hospitals, often there is no roads to their villages or houses. It might take a doctor or nurse many hours, if not days, to reach a sick person. Often they arrive too late for someone who is seriously ill. With a bicycle healthcare workers can get to families in even the most rural communities, reducing the time required to reach patients with life-saving treatment.

Having access to doctors and hospitals is something we take for granted, but it's a rarity for most people in the world. In fact, only one in seven people has the opportunity to see a doctor when they are sick. Think about seven of your friends, then imagine that only one of you could see a doctor or get needed medicine — ever! Many illnesses could be prevented, and many lives saved, if only everyone had access to treatment as well as information about how to stay healthy. For example: pregnant women would be checked during pregnancy and get help during labor — which means that many more moms and babies would survive childbirth.

Health and poverty* are a vicious circle. A person who is poor cannot afford healthcare; but illness also forces many people into poverty

# HEALTHCARE

because they can't go to work anymore or need to pay expensive medical bills. The right to receive health care is a human right. But not every country is willing or able to provide it for their citizens — not even many developed countries. With more people on Earth living longer than previous generations, the health-care situation becomes even more difficult.

Over the past 20 years impressive progress has been achieved in preventing and treating serious illnesses and reducing the number of children that die before their fifth birthday. With education*, government support and the help of effective not-for-profit organizations, many more people will benefit from access to doctors and medication in the future.

## mHealth

Mobile devices such as mobile phones are a very important tool in healthcare. There are six billion mobile phones in the world, and through text messages and voice communication many lives can be saved. Information about disease* prevention, diagnosis, or disease* outbreaks or about pregnancy, childbirth and newborn care are crucial for millions of people that don't have any other access to health care.

**What you can do**

Take care of your body and stay healthy! Be a role model for friends and family members.

# CONNECT SOME DOTS

# SUPERBUGS

Is washing hands really that important for staying healthy? The answer is yes. By washing your hands, you can prevent many diseases* caused by *bacteria*, viruses, fungi, and parasites from entering your body and making you sick.

Hygiene, which means keeping your body clean, is becoming increasingly important for all of us. We trust that when we get sick there will be medicine to help us get better — but soon that may not be true anymore. The medicine we've been relying on for the past seventy years might no longer work in the future.

Take bacteria as example: in 1928 the scientist Alexander Fleming discovered the first antibiotic, called Penicillin. Antibiotics were a breakthrough in modern medicine because they cured many illnesses and prevented many deaths caused by bacterial infections. Soon, however, these drugs may no longer be efficient. Bacteria have been on Earth for about 3.5 billon years. That means they were able to evolve and survive over this long period of time. It also means that the bacteria that make us sick are able to change their genes quite quickly and they can develop resistance to certain drugs. This way the drugs are no longer able to fight the germs. When microorganisms, such as bacteria, become resistant to drugs, the organism is called Superbug or Multiple Drug Resistant (MDR).

# SUPERBUGS

Because antibiotics do such an amazing job in curing some illnesses, people may mistakenly use them to treat diseases that aren't even caused by bacteria, but by other organisms like viruses or fungi. Other people may use them correctly, but stop taking them before the bacteria is fully killed, because they are feeling better. Overuse and wrong dosage cause the bacteria to develop resistance.

Meat production also contributes to the development of superbugs. Animals like chicken or cows are often treated with antibiotics even if they aren't sick, to improve their growth and ability to produce food. Traces of these antibiotics make their way to humans via our groundwater and the meat, eggs or milk we consume.

Strict rules for the use of antibiotics and other medicines are urgently needed. Or we will return to the days when illnesses like the flu could kill millions of people.

## Hygiene

Only 150 years ago a physician named Ignaz Semmelweiss discovered that washing hands before child birth or surgery greatly reduced patients' *mortality*. It took many more years before doctors finally accepted that hygiene is essential to prevent illness.

## What you can do

Wash your hands with regular — not antibacterial — soap and water several times every day. Discuss with your parents and your doctor if the use of antibiotics for an illness is really necessary. Eat less meat and buy organic instead.

# CONNECT SOME DOTS

# CHAPTER 2
# PLANET

# MELTING ICE CAPS

The kayak, a one-person boat with a paddle, was invented by the Inuit. The Inuit are Native people that live in Canada, Alaska, and Greenland. They used kayaks made of driftwood or whalebone, and covered with stretched animal skins, for hunting fish, seals, and whales with harpoons. The Inuit have inhabited the icy tundra for four thousand years, living in igloos and hunting in the vast Arctic ice. Now their habitat, and that of other living creatures in the Arctic and Antarctic, is endangered.

Temperatures on Earth are rising about 1.1 degrees Fahrenheit per year — at the North and South Poles the rate is even higher. Experts predict that the Arctic could be ice-free in the summer months by 2040. As the vast ice areas continue to melt, their ecosystems will become unbalanced, and many animals such as the Polar Bear may become extinct. Sea levels all over the world will rise, resulting in flooding of coastal areas. Glaciers, the icy layer that cools down Earth, will no longer be there.

Watching the ice caps melting is a sure sign that it is getting warmer on our planet. Even though some may think it's great when it's warm outside, the underlying problem, called climate change, is very bad for the Earth. Climate change means that it will be hotter in some areas, but everything will get more extreme — there will be more hurricanes, severe snowstorms, and droughts as well.

# MELTING ICE CAPS

Global Goal
### #13

*Protect
the Planet*

Climate change is caused by *greenhouse gases* that are released into the air when we burn fuel to power our cars and airplanes, or to provide electricity for our factories and homes. The more energy we consume, the more we damage our Earth. More greenhouse gases keep more of the sun's heat trapped in our atmosphere. Think about how the sun heats up a car to get a better understanding of how greenhouse gases lock the suns heat on Earth.

Solutions to reduce climate change are available now: renewable energy like solar, wind and water power; energy-efficient buildings; and electric cars are just some examples. In order to save our planet and humanity from more severe weather*, loss of biodiversity, and rising sea levels, those solutions must be implemented quickly. No problem on Earth is or ever was as urgent as climate change — it affects all living things on the planet!

## Ice Age

Climate change has happened since Earth was formed. There have been many Ice Ages when the Earth was far colder than it is now. What is different now is the speed at which the temperature is changing. It is changing ten times faster than at any time in history, and experts believe it is going to warm up twenty times as fast in the coming century.

**What you can do**

Reduce your *Carbon Footprint* by using less energy. Initiate a "Low Carbon Day" in school. Encourage your family and your school to save energy for example by using LED light bulbs, unplugging phone chargers when not in use or by not keeping appliances on standby mode.

# CONNECT SOME DOTS

# SEVERE WEATHER

Do you have a flashlight at home? Flashlights are fun to play with in the dark, but they're especially important to have as part of your home's emergency kit, in case the power goes out. Loss of electricity can happen when a hurricane, blizzard, tornado or flooding hits an area.

For people all over the world — in developed but especially in *developing countries* — extreme weather can be much more serious than losing power. Extreme weather means weather that has the potential to cause damage, interrupt a community's livelihood, and endanger human and animal life.

In recent years heavy rains and flooding, long-lasting droughts, and powerful storms that hit populated land have become much more frequent. Like the melting ice caps* you've heard about in the previous article — more severe weather is also an effect of climate change. The warmer air in the atmosphere, combined with more moisture that evaporates from warmer oceans, changes our weather pattern. Due to severe weather many people might lose their homes, their harvests or their jobs. Whole communities might have to relocate because of flooded or deserted lands. Stronger winter or hotter summers will increase the energy needs for heating or air conditioning. Heat or cold waves even kill thousands of people that don't have a shelter to be safe.

# SEVERE WEATHER

Climate change will significantly change our lives. Experts predict that about half of all currently existing plants and about one third of animals will disappear by 2080. Providing every human with food and clean water will become even more difficult, diseases* will increase, and people will have a hard time earning money in decent jobs.

Fighting climate change and fighting poverty are the most urgent tasks all humans have for the next few years. As climate change has already begun, we must quickly find ways to deal with its impacts. Early warning systems, shelters, water storage facilities, structures to prevent flooding and land erosions, and reforestation are all ways to deal with severe weather.

## What you can do

Get informed about climate change and actions you can take to help stop it. For example join tree planting initiatives. Don't waste water. Eat less meat. Make sure your family prepares and, if necessary, moves to a safe place if a hurricane or other severe weather is forecasted.

## The Ozone Hole

About 30 years ago people all over the world were scared of a severe environmental crisis caused by a chemical that was about to destroy the atmosphere's *ozone layer*. In a joint effort by all countries those chemicals were banned from products such as hair sprays or refrigerators worldwide. Slowly the ozone layer started to heal and experts say that it's hole will be closed by 2050. If the world unites to fight a global problem — change can happen!

# CONNECT SOME DOTS

# OCEAN ACIDIFICATION

Pearls are considered rare and precious. They have been used to make fine jewelry for many centuries, and people pay a lot of money for the finest quality natural pearls. Soon the value of these gemstones might rise even more because the way pearls are produced is threatened. A pearl grows from calcium carbonate (a combination of minerals and oxygen) in ocean animals such as clams, conch shells, and oysters.

The reason why there will be less natural pearls is directly linked to climate change. Besides melting arctic ice* and severe weather* (see previous articles), there is a third major effect of Climate Change and this one is affecting the Earth's oceans. Climate change causing *greenhouse gases* that are released by humans' activity into the air are absorbed by the oceans. For years experts considered that a good thing because it seemed to slow down the process of climate change. However, new studies show that greenhouse gases in the oceans turn the water acidic — sort of like if you'd pour vinegar or lemon juice into the sea.

The effects of ocean acidification are especially bad for animals that have shells or live in shells — like clams, oysters, crabs, lobsters, urchins, or snails. If these animals can't survive because their shells are dissolved in the acidic water, the animals that

# OCEAN ACIDIFICATION

Global Goal
#13

*Protect
the Planet*

feed of off shell creatures can't survive either. Then the entire *ecosystem* gets out of balance. Coral is also at risk, and with it the entire biodiversity around coral reefs.

Oceans are essential for life on Earth. Ocean fish are an important source of protein and half of all the oxygen in our atmosphere is contributed by *plankton* that live on the oceans' surfaces.

Scientists are testing ways to slow down the process of ocean acidification. It seems, though, that decreasing the amount of greenhouse gases that are released into the atmosphere is the only solution for sustaining a rich biodiversity on our planet and for making sure that there is enough oxygen for all living beings.

## Naked Eggs

Make an experiment to see the effects of acidic water on shells. An egg shell is made of the same material as a snail's shell. To study water acidification, take an egg, put it in a bowl, add enough white vinegar to cover it, and leave it overnight. The next day take it out carefully with a spoon and observe what has happened to its shell.

**What you can do**

Spread the word about climate change and how people and governments can help make a difference by releasing fewer greenhouse gases into the atmosphere.

# CONNECT SOME DOTS

# ENERGY CRISIS

Do you take a sweater along when you go to a restaurant in the summer? How about in the winter? Do you prefer wearing just a short sleeve t-shirt in the house when it is freezing cold outside? The reason people dress opposite to what the weather dictates is because of overuse of heating and air conditioning inside our houses, schools, shops, cars, and other spaces.

We use vast amounts of energy to cool and heat our houses. In fact, the United States uses more electricity for air conditioning than what all people in the entire continent of Africa use for everything that is powered by electricity. More severe weather* as a result of climate change, combined with a growing world population will contribute to exploding demands for energy in the coming years.

Most of the energy we use still comes from non-renewable sources. Those are so-called fossil fuels like coal, crude oil, and natural gas that were formed over 300 million years ago. Uranium is another form of non-renewable energy. It is used for *nuclear power.*

Fossil fuels will become very scarce at some point in the future, and because only some countries can extract them from the earth, people will fight even more wars for access to them. Burning fossil fuels also has a very negative impact on the environment and is a major contributor to climate change.

# ENERGY CRISIS

A way to cope with this growing energy crisis is to find efficient ways to use renewable energy sources such as wind, sun, water, heat from the earth's center, animal waste, and plant materials. Those can be converted to solar energy, hydropower, geothermal heating, or biogas. Eleven percent of the world's energy consumption already comes from renewable sources. Progress in developing more efficient and sustainable energy technologies might enable people around the world to use less fossil fuel and make "energy for all" a reality.

## Fracking

Hydraulic fracturing, called fracking is a method of extracting natural gas from the earth to use as fossil fuel. The process involves drilling deep holes into the Earth's surface and pumping chemicals with high pressure through those holes that break the stones that hold the gas. During the process huge amounts of greenhouse gases are released, ground waters are polluted, lots of water is wasted and the likelyhood of earth quakes is increased.

## What you can do

Switch off appliances, lights, heaters, and air conditioners if you don't need them. Set the temperature of your cooling unit a few degrees higher in hot weather and a few degrees lower in cold weather. Wear your sweater during the right season!

# CONNECT SOME DOTS

# OVERCONSUMPTION

On average, every person uses 130 plastic bags per year. Plastic bags are very harmful to the environment because plastic doesn't decompose and is a big part of our *landfill*. It is of little value for recycling and it is made from the non-renewable natural resource petroleum. We know that we should replace plastic bags by reusable ones. But what about changing what and how much we shop and put in those bags?

People buy things to fulfill their needs and wants. Needs are satisfied if humans have food, shelter, clothes, and medicine. Wants, on the other hand, can be endless. They are things we don't actually need but would be nice to have — new sneakers, another toy, fancy clothes, the latest phones or tablets. All of these products require Earth's resources, such as oil, natural gas, water, or wood. In the past thirty years alone, we have consumed almost a third of all our planet's resources. Most of them can't be renewed. With a world population of nine billion people by 2030, solutions to keep up with growing demand for resources must be found quickly.

One solution is to convince people to buy less. Another solution is to change the way products are made. Manufacturers must come up with ways to reuse and recycle every material. Right now most products are thrown away within six months. In a

# OVERCONSUMPTION

**Global Goal #12**

*Responsible Consumption*

revolutionary new concept called "Circular Economy," no goods are wasted; instead, every product, component and material is reused to make new products. For example, in a circular economy, a sweater would be made with recycled wool, and thread and reused buttons; the sewing machine would be solar-powered. When the buyer no longer wanted the sweater, he'd return it to the manufacturer, who would either resell it as second-hand, reuse buttons and threads again or recycle the fabric for other uses like cleaning cloths or insulation materials. At last if resell, reuse, recycle are no options the materials are used for producing energy.

While Earth may not run out of natural resources, they will become increasingly scarce if we don't solve the problem of overconsumption. When that happens, only a few fortunate people will be able to afford them.

## Planned obsolescence

To make more profits, many companies design products to break, wear out, or be outdated after a short while. The old products get thrown away and new products are bought each time at the expense of Earth's resources and environment.

## What you can do

When you are about to buy a new toy, gadget, or piece of clothing, ask yourself if you really need it. Maybe you can borrow the product from a friend or neighbor through a new concept called "sharing economy". Or buy products that have been made from recycled materials.

# CONNECT SOME DOTS

# OVERFISHING

Most of us think of a fisherman as a guy in rubber pants and rubber boots holding a fishing rod and a net to catch fish he either eats himself or sells to make a living. The fisherman of our imagination knows when and how to hunt for specific species and respects the oceans so that his catch will be guaranteed for many years to come.

Modern fishing has nothing to do with this ideal. High-tech vessels as big as football fields stay out on the ocean for months, fishing, processing, and freezing fish on board. They use miles-long lines and huge nets that trawl along the ocean floors. These fishing fleets are so big, one can see their lights from space. They even use satellite navigation to find fish.

With all the fishing equipment that exists on Earth we could fish on four Earth-like planets. But we only have one Earth and only five oceans, which will eventually be empty if humans continue to fish as much as they currently do, because our modern fishing methods destroy the marine ecosystem. Some experts estimate that on average only 60 percent, but in some cases — for example in shrimp fishing — only a tenth of what is caught is eaten by humans or their pets. The rest consists of fish waste and by-catch, such as other fish species, turtles or dolphins that are accidentally caught and killed.

Overfishing means humans catch so many fish in such a short time that nature can't keep up restoring the fish population. Ninety

# OVERFISHING

percent of the world's large predatory fish like tuna and shark have already been killed. And you know that when pieces in a food web are missing, the whole system is threatened to collapse.

We need healthy ocean ecosystems. Half the oxygen in our atmosphere is provided by oceans and fish are a vital food source. Yet only one percent of all oceans are protected from fishing and oil drilling. There are amazing organizations such as Pristine Seas and individuals that are working on solutions to stop overfishing. The creation of marine parks provides large protected areas where fish can breed and thrive. Marine parks, high tech-satellite monitoring and sustainable aqua farming are other ways to protect the oceans. We all must be aware of the dangers of destroying our ecosystems and governments must play a key role in protecting the oceans. Healthy oceans make all humans better off — not just fishermen.

## What you can do

Make sure the seafood you eat is caught in a sustainable way by checking fish shopping guides and eat fish in moderation. Spread the word about the overfishing problem among your friends and classmates.

## Ghost Fishing

Industrial fishing vessels often lose their huge nets in the open oceans. These nets keep moving along and catch and kill fish over many decades without anyone ever seeing them again.

# CONNECT SOME DOTS

# ENDANGERED ANIMALS

Balloons belong to a birthday party like cake and presents. Releasing balloons into the sky is a symbol of good luck, and we humans set free about one billion balloons each year.

Unfortunately, balloons eventually pop and fall back to Earth, where they litter the ground and pose a threat to animals. Cows, dogs, birds, and especially marine animals like dolphins, whales, and turtles are often hurt or killed by balloons. Sea turtles, for example, mistake popped balloons for jellyfish, then swallow the material and die a slow death from blocked stomachs. Sea turtles are endangered, which means they are at risk of going extinct.

Litter and pollution are but one of the many ways humans threaten the survival of plants and animals. Another is habitat loss. Rainforests are cut down to create fields for agriculture; much of the natural land is consumed by ever-growing cities. Other reasons animals are endangered include hunting and disease, which can occur when humans introduce new species into a previously stable ecosystem. The biggest threat, however, is climate change — bringing destruction like melting ice in the Arctic, warmer oceans, and droughts in grasslands.

Scientists estimate that 40% of all animal species are endangered. They include tigers, Java Rhinos and Giant Pandas. Many plants

# ENDANGERED ANIMALS

Global Goal

#15

Life
on Land

and animals — like dinosaurs and mammoths — have gone extinct over the millions of years life has existed on Earth. Yet over the last three hundred years, the rate at which species have vanished from Earth has drastically increased due to humans' actions.

The good news is that there are many people working hard to solve the problem. Efforts include conservation projects, lobbying to convince governments and corporations to protect wildlife through national parks and other protected areas, re-planting forests and other ecosystems, introducing laws to prevent hunting, and raising animals in conservation centers or zoos to later release them into the wild.

These efforts require the help and support of all humans. Healthy ecosystems are essential to our lives. They help regulate our climate and provide clean air and water, fertile soils, food, medicines, and building and clothing materials. And we all agree, that animals make our lives richer in so many ways.

## Endangered Sharks

One third of all sharks that live in the open ocean will probably go extinct. Marine biologists believe that the incredible amount of about 70-100 million sharks are killed each year because people want to use their fins.

**What you can do**

Support animal conservation organizations. Recycle and use recycled products, save energy, buy sustainable products, and educate friends about helping wildlife. If you live close to a forest or beach, spend a few afternoons each month picking up trash.

# CONNECT SOME DOTS

# DEFORESTATION

A Native American proverb says, "We do not inherit the earth from our ancestors, we borrow it from our children." Yet our generations destroy the earth we have borrowed in many ways, and at a massive speed.

One example of large-scale damage is the destruction of the world's forests. Forests are cut down to make paper or wood products out of trees, to plant large fields of palm trees for palm oil production, or to increase the amount of land that can be used for agriculture.

Think about your day: you've probably used paper for writing, drawing or crafting, read a book, wiped your mouth on a napkin, sat on a chair, and walked on a wooden floor. You may also have washed your hair with shampoo, and maybe you ate some ice cream — products that were made with palm oil. There are hundreds of examples of goods for which trees are cut down. Together with unintended deforestation — that is accidental loss of trees due to wildfires or animals grazing on small trees — a forest the size of two football fields vanishes every minute. If this damage continues at the same rate there won't be any forests left in about a hundred years.

Forests are essential for life on Earth. They provide us with half of the oxygen we breathe, and they are home to almost ninety

# DEFORESTATION

percent of all land-based animals and plants on our planet. They help maintain the Earth's water cycle and they prevent soil from being flushed away when there is a lot of rain. Trees are also very important in the fight against climate change because they turn *greenhouse gases* into oxygen.

Planting new trees is one way to fight the harsh effects of deforestation, but that is just a small step that can't keep up with the speed of destruction. "Reduce, Reuse, Recycle" initiatives also help. However, the only real solution is for governments to start protecting large parts of their forests from being cut down, and to carefully manage the way trees are cut in other parts.

## Wangaris Trees

Wangari Maathai, a woman from the African country of Kenya, is called "The Mother of Trees." She received the *Nobel Peace Prize* in 2004 for her Greenbelt Movement, which planted 30 million trees in the deforested areas of her homeland.

**What you can do**

Use both sides of paper when you write or draw. Read magazines and books online. Buy recycled paper products, look for grocery brands that use certified sustainable palm oil, and ask your parents and their friends to buy furniture that is made from reclaimed or certified wood.

# CONNECT SOME DOTS

Energy Crisis

Sustainable Agriculture

Urbanization

Inequality

Food Waste

Deforestation

Endangered Animals

Severe Weather

Ocean Acidification

Water Access

# ENERGY POVERTY

Dinner is cooked on a stove, which is generally powered by gas or electricity. There is an exhaust vent right above the cooking area to prevent smoke from getting into your house. And when the cooking is finished, you can simply switch off the appliance and be done.

What if people don't have electricity or a safe gas line to power modern cooking tools? In *developing countries*, three billion people cook their food with so-called biomass — that is wood, charcoal, or animal dung — over open fireplaces. Using this kind of energy is bad for many reasons: the wood and charcoal are often obtained in ways that severely hurt the environment — think about deforestation*. The smoke from burning wood and coal in open fireplaces gets into the atmosphere and contributes to climate change. And burning biomass pollutes the air inside a house; every day thousands of people get sick or die from the toxic fumes. There is no other cause in the world that kills more people than inhaling smoke from these fires — four million people die every year. Women and girls suffer the most because they are the ones who spend many hours a day collecting the biomass and cooking the food for the family while breathing highly polluted air*.

# ENERGY POVERTY

Global Goal
## #7

*Clean Energy*

When individuals and communities don't have access to modern energy services, it is called Energy Poverty. Can you think of how your life would be affected if you didn't have access to electricity? Not being able to cook is just one aspect. Without electricity there is no modern healthcare*, no heating or cooling, no light, no computers or Internet, and no powered farming or manufacturing tools.

Organizations and governments are working hard to find ways to bring energy to all seven billion people in the world by the year 2030, and to solve one of the world's most urgent health and environmental problems. The challenge is to provide reliable supplies of energy to help people escape poverty and illness while simultaneously protecting our environment.

## Soccer for light

Among the many projects to bring electricity to the energy poor is a soccer ball. A little generator inside the ball charges a battery that then can power up to three lamps. Playing half an hour of soccer provides three hours of light. What a good excuse for students to first play soccer and then do homework![1]

## What you can do

Raise money to support innovative energy projects such as energy creating soccer balls. Participate in a school science fair with your ideas for energy solutions. Save energy by switching off appliances and lights.

# CONNECT SOME DOTS

# AIR POLLUTION

Have you ever seen this sign and do you know what it means? It means "No Idling" and it is supposed to keep drivers from letting their cars run when they are not driving.

Cars produce more air pollution than any other human activity. Almost all cars on the road today are powered by burning gasoline. Gasoline is a fossil fuel, which releases pollutants into the air that are very harmful to humans and the environment. It doesn't matter if a vehicle is moving or standing — an idling car releases as much pollution as one that is moving.

Air Pollution means that harmful gases get into the Earth's atmosphere causing breathing problems and diseases* for humans and animals. Millions of people die each year because they breathe in polluted air. Acid rain that poisons plants and *greenhouse gases* that are responsible for Climate Change are other severe effects of air pollution.

Natural and non-human events can also pollute the air, such as volcanic eruptions, wildfires, or sand storms. However, humans are responsible for making air pollution the largest single danger for the environment. To produce goods or burn waste, different industries release lots of smoke. Through the use of pesticides and fertilizers in agriculture and gardening, many dangerous chemicals get into the air. And household products such as cleaners or paints

# AIR POLLUTION

pose great risks to a house's indoor air quality — as does cooking over open fireplaces with biomass. Yet the biggest polluter is transportation: Cars, ships, and airplanes are powered by burning fossil fuels, and their emissions severely harm our atmosphere.

Cleaning up the air is extremely difficult, if not impossible. The goal of governments, companies, and individuals must be to prevent harmful gases from being emitted into the air. One major solution is using sustainable energy sources such as wind, water and solar power, and alternative forms of transportation such as bikes or buses. In Copenhagen, Denmark, for example, already one third of citizens bike to work and school every day. Everyone can join in to help solve Earth's air pollution problem.

## Smog

Smog is a word made up of Smoke and Fog. It describes the dirty air in cities. Smog alerts warn people to stay inside on days when smog is particularly bad. In some cities in Asia, smog sometimes gets so dense that people can't see further than a few hundred yards.

## What you can do

Ask your parents to use their car less, and to turn of the motor when the car is parked. Use mass transportation, such as a bus, or walk or bike to get to places. Educate others about the dangers of air pollution.

# CONNECT SOME DOTS

# SUSTAINABLE AGRICULTURE

If you have a flyswatter at home you probably don't like insects that much. But think about how useful they are. Ladybugs, for example, eat plant-harming aphids. Beetles and crickets are decomposers that turn animal dung or dead wood into soil. Bees make honey and pollinate plants so they can grow. There is many different benefits we get from bugs — but one has yet to be accepted: Insects as humans' protein source of the future.

Protein is a nutrient that is essential for our bodies. As the Earth's population is predicted to be nine billion people by 2050, there may not be enough animal protein the way we know it today. Scientists therefore see insects like locusts or worms as important parts of our diets.

Providing nutritious food for the increasing number of humans while decreasing the impact of food production on our environment will be a huge challenge. The way most of the world's food is produced today has a very negative effect on our planet, our health, animal welfare and many communities. Producing meat and crops consumes vast amounts of water; cows release *greenhouse gases* into the atmosphere; cattle and chickens are often kept in tiny enclosures and fed with hormones. In addition, plants are sprayed with pesticides, forests are cut down to create

# SUSTAINABLE AGRICULTURE

Global Goal
## #2

*No
Hunger*

agricultural land, rivers and lakes are polluted with animal wastes and fertilizers; and many chemicals are used to preserve foods until they reach the consumer.

There are many *sustainable* solutions to these problems — solutions that protect the environment as well as the health of humans and animals. Crops that grow back every year, bugs that fight pests, soil protection techniques, shade-providing trees, and financial and technological support for small-scale farmers are just some approaches.

Experts are convinced that sustainable agriculture, along with more equal distribution of food and the reduction of food waste, will provide a better way to feed the world while preventing the earth from cooking.[1]

## Rooftop veggies

Almost half the world's population lives in towns and cities. Providing all those people with fresh and locally grown produce is difficult. There simply is no space for farming. That's why a growing number of buildings are using their rooftops for gardening. Imagine if there were a strawberry or potato field on every high-rise in your town!

**What you can do**

Ask your parents to buy from local farmers and when possible to pick organic foods and produce that is in season. Grow your own herbs and vegetables at home or in a community garden. Spread the word about sustainable food production.

# CONNECT SOME DOTS

# CHAPTER 3
# ONE EARTH

# ALL IN ONE BOAT

A wise man from Singapore[1] compared the countries of the world with a cruise ship. He said that in the past people lived in 193 different "boats" — that's how many countries there are in the world[2]. Each boat had a captain and crew who set the rules and made sure their boat didn't collide with others. Now that the world has become so connected and its countries so dependent on each other, it is as if the people from the 193 countries live in one big boat with 193 different cabins. Everyone on board must learn to get along. They have to agree on the direction the ship is heading, and they must agree not to destroy the boat they all share.

Think about what would happen if a few cabins locked their doors and refused to communicate with everyone else. What if those cabins had the keys for the kitchen, fuel for the engines, or medical supplies? What if the people in one cabin decided to cook on open fires? What if people in others started fighting with each other? What if residents of one cabin poured toxic waste in the ship's water supply? What if someone in a cabin became ill with an infectious disease?

Aboard this giant ship, what the people of one cabin do affects everyone else on board, in both good and bad ways. The same is

# ALL IN ONE BOAT

true for each country in the world. Countries can no longer pretend that what happens elsewhere in the world doesn't affect them.

The world is interconnected: its economies, currencies, food supplies, and the trade of its natural resources. International alliances such as the *United Nations* or *NATO* demand that countries help each other if there is a war. Diseases travel around the globe faster than they might be detected. Through the Internet, people all over the world get real-time information about what is happing in other countries. And damage to the environment affects all of us. Everything you read about in this book impacts everyone in the world, no matter in which country they live. We need to remember that we are all in one boat, and we must not destroy it.

## Global Citizen

Being global citizens means being citizens of the world who know that they are part of one community. It means being aware that everything they do has an impact on the whole planet and all its people. Global citizens, no matter their age, know that they can make a difference in the world!

## What you can do

Learn as much as you can about the world and its challenges. Be respectful and mindful of every person, animal, and the environment. Discuss with your friends what it means to be a global citizen and how all of you can join to make the world a better place.

# SUSTAINABLE DEVELOPMENT GOALS

To solve major world problems such as hunger and climate change, the *United Nations* have adopted 17 Global Goals, also called the **Sustainable Development Goals** in September 2015. With these goals countries all over the world will commit to ending extreme poverty, protect the planet, and make sure all people can make a decent and healthy living.

Every human, on Earth, young and old, rich and poor, is asked to learn about these goals and to help achieve them.

### #1 No Poverty
End poverty in all its forms everywhere.

### #2 No Hunger
End hunger, achieve food security and improved nutrition and promote sustainable agriculture.

### #3 Good Health
Ensure healthy lives and promote well-being for all at all ages.

### #4 Quality Education
Ensure inclusive and equitable quality education and promote lifelong learning opportunities for all.

# SUSTAINABLE DEVELOPMENT GOALS

 **#5 Gender Equality**
Achieve gender equality and empower all women and girls.

 **#6 Clean Water And Sanitation**
Ensure availability and sustainable management of water and sanitation for all.

 **#7 Clean Energy**
Ensure access to affordable, reliable, sustainable and modern energy for all.

 **#8 Good Jobs and Economic Growth**
Promote sustained, inclusive and sustainable economic growth, full and productive employment and decent work for all.

 **#9 Innovation and Infrastructure**
Build resilient infrastructure, promote inclusive and sustainable industrialization and foster innovation.

 **#10 Reduced Inequalities**
Reduce inequality within and among countries.

 **#11 Sustainable Cities and Communities**
Make cities and human settlements inclusive, safe, resilient and sustainable.

# SUSTAINABLE DEVELOPMENT GOALS

**#12 Responsible Consumption**
Ensure sustainable consumption and production patterns.

**#13 Protect the Planet**
Take urgent action to combat climate change and its impacts.

**#14 Life below Water**
Conserve and sustainably use the oceans, seas and marine resources for sustainable development.

**#15 Life on Land**
Protect, restore and promote sustainable use of terrestrial ecosystems, sustainably manage forests, combat desertification, and halt and reverse land degradation and halt biodiversity loss.

**#16 Peace and Justice**
Promote peaceful and inclusive societies for sustainable development, provide access to justice for all and build effective, accountable and inclusive institutions at all levels.

**#17 Partnerships for the Goals**
Strengthen the means of implementation and revitalize the global partnership for sustainable development.

# STORIES OF HOPE

Many wonderful initiatives are started to help make this world a better place — by adults and children alike! Here are just four examples of how everyone can make a difference:

### Selling lemonade to fight slavery
Vivienne Harr was eight years old when she started a lemonade stand to raise money for Not For Sale, a not-for-profit organization that helps fight human trafficking. She raised over $100,000 for the cause. Her campaign became a business, and "Make a Stand Lemon-Aid," her organic lemonade, is now sold in 137 stores, generating money to end modern-day slavery.

### Planting trees to value girls
In the village community of Piplantri, India, girls used to be valued far less than boys. However, the village has started a new tradition. Every time a girl is born the community plants 111 trees. They also raise money for the girl's family, which they will receive in 20 years if the girl is able to finish school and is not married at a young age. With this initiative many good things are achieved all at once: the village helps the environment by planting trees, guaranteeing income for the family that can harvest the fruits. They help girls receive an education and reach the age of 18 before getting married. But most of all, they create a change in how girls are valued.

# STORIES OF HOPE

### Knitting against poverty
Helping women in Uganda make a living was the idea of three college boys who liked knitting. They started teaching women living in refugee camps how to crochet, in order to give them a means of breaking the cycle of poverty. They provided the women with yarn and paid a decent salary for their work. Today, over 150 people in Uganda and Peru are working, receiving an education, and being mentored toward a brighter future by the organization Krochet Kids.

### Teddy Bears for Comfort
After the horrible earthquake in Haiti in 2010, a boy from Michigan began collecting teddy bears to send to children who had lost their homes in the disaster. Blare Gooch sent nearly 50,000 bears to children in need of comfort. He has now begun raising toy and school supply donations as well.

*Send us your story of hope to [33storiesofhope@whyzz.com](mailto:33storiesofhope@whyzz.com) and we will publish your initiative on our website.*

# GLOSSARY

### Abuse
Abuse is any action that intentionally harms another person. It can be physical (with violence) or mental (with words).

### Abolitionist Movement
A social or political movement aimed at ending slavery. In the United States, abolitionists advocated an end to end slavery in the decades leading up to the Civil War, with the belief that "all men are created equal."

### Animal Welfare
The well-being of animals: ensuring they are free from thirst, hunger, pain, injury, disease, fear, and distress. Animal welfare is especially important in activities humans are involved in, such as farming, zoos, research, or pet keeping.

### Atrocity
A very cruel or terrible act or action.

### Bacteria
A tiny living organism, the simplest form of life. Bacteria can be found everywhere and are very important for Earth's biodiversity. Some bacteria can make humans sick; most, however, are helpful.

### Citizenship
A citizen is a member of a country, community or group. A citizen generally has certain rights and responsibilities within their community.

### Developing country
A country that has relatively limited infrastructure such as streets, railroads, or electricity, and where people often earn little money and lack sufficient access to healthcare or nutritious food.

# GLOSSARY

### Ecosystem

A self-sustaining habitat in which plants, animals, and microorganisms live in balance with non-living things like light (or sunlight), soil, and the water cycle.

### Epidemic

A disease that affects many people and that spreads quickly over a wide area such as a country or continent.

### Greenhouse Gas

Greenhouses gases hold the sun's heat in the atmosphere and help to maintain a reasonable temperature on Earth during the night. Carbon dioxide is the main greenhouse gas; others, for example water vapor, also add to the Greenhouse Effect. If there is too high a concentration of these gases, Earth becomes too warm because less heat can be released back into space. Humans emit greenhouse gases, especially carbon dioxide, with everyday activities such as driving cars, flying airplanes or raising cattle.

### Hyperconnectivity

Because of the Internet, mobile technology, and the Internet of things, everything — people, places, things, companies, and governments — will be increasingly connected.

### Land Degradation

The process by which land becomes arid and unusable due to extreme weather, urbanization, deforestation, or poor farming practices.

### Landfill

A word for garbage dump.

### Mortality

The number of people who die from a certain cause like disease, war, or malnutrition.

# GLOSSARY

### NATO
The North Atlantic Treaty Organization. Formed after World War II in 1949, it is a consortium of 19 countries that has agreed to help defend each other in the event that any member country is attacked.

### Nobel Peace Prize
One of five awards created by Alfred Nobel to recognize people for outstanding achievements. The Nobel Peace Prize recognizes individuals who have contributed to long-term peace between countries.

### Nuclear Energy
Energy in the nucleus (core) of a uranium atom. Atoms are tiny particles that are the basis for every object on our planet. If the nucleus of an atom is broken, the energy inside it is released. Uranium is a metallic element in the earth's crust and is considered a non-renewable energy source.

### Sustainable
If something is used, produced, developed in a sustainable way than the object or the resources to produce aren't depleted, and can therefore last for a long time.

### Trauma
Long-term mental or emotional effects resulting from a horrible or very difficult experience. These include nightmares, anxieties, or depression. A trauma is also the term used if a person's body is seriously injured.

### United Nations
Organization founded in 1945 with the goal of helping the various countries in the world support each other and live together in peace. One hundred and ninety-three countries (out of 197) are members of the U.N. Sub-groups include UNHCR, which helps refugees, UNICEF, which supports children worldwide, and the International Court of Justice, which resolves conflicts between countries.

# SOURCES

## 5 quarters (Poverty)

Ending Extreme Poverty, Global Monitoring Report, The World Bank, Worldbank.org © 2015 The World Bank Group

Extreme Poverty, Trickleup.com, © 2015 TrickleUp

Millenium Development Goals, Goal 1: Eradicate Extreme Poverty and Hunger by 2015, The World Bank, worldbank.org, © 2015 The World Bank Group

Unicef, Millennium Development Goals, Goal 1: Eradicate Extreme Poverty and Hunger, UNICEF, Unicef.org, © UNICEF/HQ98-0891/Pirozzi

## Globe (Inequality)

Economic and Social Affairs, United Nations, NY 2013, UN.org

Inequality Matters, Report on the World Social Situation 2013, United Nations

Social Inclusion, The World Bank, August 15, 2013, Worldbank.org © 2015 The World Bank Group

Unicef, Sustainable Development starts and ends with safe, healthy and well educated children, Unicef.org, May 2013, © UNICEF

## Pajamas (Homelessness)

American Psychological Association, Effects of Poverty, Hunger and Homelessness, Apa.org, © 2015 American Psychological Association

Glennie, Jonathan, Homelessness: A tragic form of poverty, Theguardian.com, December 15, 2010, © 2015 Guardian News and Media Limited or its affiliated companies

What is homelessness? National Alliance to end homelessness, © copyright 2015, published on whyzz.com

Wikipedia, Homelessness, Wikipedia.org

## Peanut Butter (Malnutrition)

[1]"PB&J is A-OK". *Prepared Foods 171.10 (): p.32(1).* Prepared Foods. Oct 2002

Mc Arthur, John, The Hunger Game, Foreign Affairs.com, June 16, 2015, © 2015 Council on Foreign Relations, Inc. All Rights Reserved

Project Peanut Butter, Copyright © 2015

# SOURCES

UNICEF, Celebrating nutrition achievements in Wolaita, Getachew, Indrias, MANCHA, Ethiopia, Unicef.org, August 9 2013, Copyright © UNICEF

Sustainable Future, Unesco.org, Copyright © UNESCO, 2010

UNESCO, Hunger and malnutrition in the world, Teaching and Learning for a Sustainable Future

Wikipedia, Hunger, Wikipedia.org

World Food Programme, Hunger, Wfp.org, 2015 © World Food Programme

Unesco.org, Copyright © UNESCO, 2010

## Birth Certificate (Identity)

Handfield, Laurel What is a birth certificate?, Whyzz.com, © Whyzz LLC 2015

Niedermaier, Constanze, 33 Things to Explain the World to Kids, 1st Edition, 2015, © Whyzz LLC 2015

UNICEF, Every Child's Birth Right, Inequities and trends in birth registration, Unicef.org, © United Nations Children's Fund (UNICEF), Data and Analytics Section, Division of Policy and Strategy, December 2013

UNICEF, Birth Registration: Right from the Start, The Innocenti Digest, Unicef.org, March 2002, © United Nations Children's Fund (UNICEF)

## Leash (Violence)

[1]United Nations committee on the Rights of the child, general comment No. 13 on the convention on the Rights of the child

Borenstein, Seth, World Becoming Less Violent: Despite Global Conflict, Statistics Show Violence In Steady Decline, The World Post, October 22, 2011, Huffingtonpost.org, Copyright ©2015 TheHuffingtonPost.com, Inc.

Dosomething.org 11 Facts About Bullying

Keim, Brandon, Is It Time to Treat Violence Like a Contagious Disease? Wired, January 18th, 2013, Copyright ©2015 Condé Nast

Kristof, Nicholas, The Giant Rats that Save Lives, New York Times, April 18th 2015, © 2015 The New York Times Company

UNICEF, Peacebuilding, Education and Advocacy Programme, Learning for Peace,Unicef.org, © United Nations Children's Fund (UNICEF), January 2014

# SOURCES

Wikipedia, Violence, Wikipedia.org, July 2015

Wright, Lindsey How Education can Prevent Violence, UNESCO In the Spotlight: Education and Culture, November 27, 2011, Unesco Education Blogspot

## Water Bottle (Terrorism)

Academic Kids Encyclopedia Definition of terrorism, AcademicKids.com, June 2005

Kidshealth, Terrorism, Kidshealth.org, January 2014, © 1995-2015 The Nemours Foundation

Wikipedia, Terrorism, Wikipedia.org

Zalman, Amy, PhD, Causes of Terrorism-Why are the Causes of Terrorism So Hard to Identify? © 2015 About.com

## Tent (Refugees)

Burke, Kevin, The Mediterranean Migrant Crisis Isn't Merely Europe's Problem to Solve, Citizens for Global Solutions, May 13th 2015, ® Citizens for Global Solutions

Nuñez, Christina, Why people migrate: 11 surprising reasons, Global Citizen, Dec. 4, 2014, Globalcitizen.org, © 2012-2015 Global Poverty Project, Inc.

United Nations, Refugees, The Numbers, UN.org, Copyright © United Nations 2015

Wikipedia, Refugee Camp, Wikipedia.org

## Shopping Cart (Food Waste)

[1]Benson, Jonathan, Daily amount of food waste in America enough to fill a football stadium, Naturalnews.com, October 17th, 2011, Natural News Network © 2015

Chipman, John, Food waste, overeating threaten global security, CBC News, November 23, 2013, Cbcnews.com, © 2015 CBC/Radio-Canada

Cornell Chronicle, U.S. could feed 800 million people with grain that livestock eat, Cornell ecologist advises animal scientists, Cornell.edu, August 7, 1997, © 2015 Cornell Chronicle

Gunders, Dana, The Ugly Truth About Food Waste In America, NPR, September 21, 2012, Npr.org, © 2015 NPR

The USGS Water School: Per capita water use: How much water do you use in your home?, water.usgs.gov

# SOURCES

### Hair Brush (Water Access)

Evans, Hugh/Moynahan, *Bridget*, Clean Water: A Simple Way to Increase Opportunity for Women and Girls, Huffington Post, March 04, 2015, Huffingtonpost.org, Copyright ©2015 TheHuffingtonPost.com, Inc.

Nuñez, Christina, We use water for EVERYTHING. Here are some examples, Global Citizen, Dec. 4, 2014, Globalcitizen.org, © 2012-2015 Global Poverty Project, Inc.

United Nations, International Water for Life Decade, UN.org, Copyright © United Nations 2015

Water.org, Water Facts, Copyright © 1990-2015 Water.org

### Toilet Brush (Sanitation)

[1]Bill Gates Names Winners of the Reinvent the Toilet Challenge, Bill and Melinda Gates Foundation, Gatesfoundation.org

[2]Listverse, 15 Fascinating Facts About Toilets, Listverse.com, Copyright © 2007–2015 Listverse Ltd

Bulletin of the World Health Organization, In the market for proper sanitation, March 3, 2010, Who.org © WHO 2015

Lewis, Tanya, 5 Ways Toilets Change the World, Livescience.com, November 19, 2013, Purch Copyright © 2015

Spears, Dean, The toilet gap: How much of differences across developing countries in child height can sanitation explain? Development Impact, The World Bank Blog, Worldbank.org, June 2, 2013, © 2015 The World Bank Group

Todd, Eloise, Fact of the day: Say YES to toilets, One.org, 2015

Water.org, Flipping the Statistics, Copyright ©1990-2015 Water.org

Water.org, 3 things most of the world can't do, Copyright © 1990-2015 Water.org

### Graduation Hat (Gender Equality)

Brewer, Holly, List of Gender Stereotypes, Copyright 2015 Healthguidance.org

TeachUnicef, Empowering Women: Empowering Children, Unicef.org, Copyright © UNICEF

# SOURCES

Ebbitt, Kathleen, The SDGs can make a real difference for women and girls, Globalcitizen.org, March 9th, 2015, © 2012-2015 Global Poverty Project, Inc.

Player, Abigail, Gender equality: why women are still held back, Theguardian.com, December 6th, 2013, © 2015 Guardian News and Media Limited

Statistics from *Miss Representation,* The Representation Project, © 2015 The Representation Project

## Wedding Cake (Child Marriage)

[1] www.girleffect.org

Girls not Brides, How can we end child marriage?, Girlsnotbrides.org

Girls not Brides, Child Marriage around the World. 20 countries with the highest rates of Child Marriage, Girlsnotbrides.org

UNICEF, Early Marriage – A Harmful Traditional Practice, Unicef.org, © The United Nations Children's Fund (UNICEF), 2005

Wilson, Michael, Who's responsible for ending child marriage in Zambia? Everyone! GlobalCitizen.org, March 10, 2015, © 2012-2015 Global Poverty Project, Inc.

## Chocolate (Child Labor)

[1] Terri Guillemets

The CNN Freedom Project, Who consumes the most chocolate?, CNN.com January 17th, 2012, © 2015 Cable News Network. Turner Broadcasting System, Inc.

Rohwetter, Marcus, Dafuermuessen Kinder schuften. Zeit Leo 2, 2015

Scholastic, Child Labor Around the World, Scholastic.com, TM ® & © 2015 Scholastic Inc.

UNICEF, Child Labour and UNICEF in Action: Children at the Centre, Unicef.org © United Nations Children's Fund (UNICEF), May 2014

Wikipedia, Child Labor, Wikipedia.org

## Passport (Modern Day Slavery)

[1] Skinner, Ben, A crime so monstrous, © 2008 Simon & Schuster, Inc.

Antislavery.org, What is Modern Slavery?

The Freedom Fund, Thefreedomfund.org

# SOURCES

The Freedom Project, Human Trafficking, Thefreedomproject.org, Copyright © 2015

U.S. Department of State, What is Modern Slavery?, State.gov

## Tire Tube (Education)

Niedermaier, Constanze, 33 Things to Explain the World to Kids, ©2015 Whyzz LLC

NBC News, Risky river crossing: Filipino kids tube to get to school, Nbcnews.com, October 12th, 2012

Solberg Erna/Brende, Børge, Why education is key to development, World Economic Forum, weforum.org, July 7th, 2015

UNICEF, Basic Education and Gender Equality, The Big Picture, unicef.org, July 23rd, 2015, © UNICEF

## Elevator Buttons (Urbanization)

Chan, Wilfred, World's fastest elevator: Like riding a train into the sky, CNN.com, April 23, 2014, © 2015 Cable News Network. Turner Broadcasting System, Inc.

The Economist, Safe Cities Index 2015 White Paper, Economist.com, Copyright © The Economist Newspaper Limited 2014

UNFPA, United Nations Population Fund, Urbanization, unfpa.org

United Nations, Department of Economic and Social Affairs, 2014 Revision of the World Urbanization Prospects, Un.org, July 10th 2014, New York, Copyright © United Nations 2015

Unplanned Urbanization in Developing Countries, 2015, weforum.org, © World Economic Forum

World Economic Forum, Global Agenda Council on Urbanization, Issue Overview, 2012, weforum.org, © World Economic Forum

World Economic Forum, Part 2: Risks in Focus: 2.3 City Limits: The Risks of Rapid and Unplanned Urbanization in Developing Countries

## Lock (Cyber Security)

Devlin Megan, What means cyber crime? Whyzz.com © Whyzz Publications LLC, 2015

University of Maryland, University College, Cybersecurity, Umuc.edu, © 2015 University of Maryland University College

# SOURCES

Homeland Security, Cybersecurity Overview, dhs.gov, April 27th, 2015

World Economic Forum, Risk and Responsibility in a Hyperconnected World, Pathways to Global Cyber Resilience, weforum.org, © World Economic Forum

## Sugar Cube (Diseases)

Gatesnotes, Child Death will go down and more diseases will be wiped out, 2015 Annual Gates Letter, Bill and Melinda Gates Foundation, Gatesnotes.com, © 2015 The Gates Notes LLC

UNICEF, Immunization, Unicef.org, © UNICEF

United Nations, Global Issues, Health, UN.org, Copyright © United Nations 2015

Wikipedia, Disease, Wikipedia.org

## Bicycle (Healthcare)

BRAC, 600 trained to reach out to the unreachable, Brac.org, Copyright ©2012 BRAC IC

Healthypeople.gov, Access to Health Services

Shah, Anup, Health Care Around the World, Global Issues, Globalissues.org, September 22nd, 2011, © Copyright 1998–2015

Tiba Foundation, Bicycles for Health Workers in Rural Africa: Simple, Inexpensive, Life-Saving, tibafoundation.org, June 2nd, 2011, Copyright © 2015 Tiba Foundation

Torgan, Allie, Bringing health care to the world's most remote areas, CNN.com, February 23rd, 2012, © 2015 Cable News Network. Turner Broadcasting System, Inc.

Wikipedia, mHealth, Wikipedia.org

## Soap (Superbugs)

CDC, Centers for Disease Control and Prevention, About Antimicrobial Resistance, Cdc.gov, September 16th, 2013

Wikipedia, Multiple Drug Resistance, Wikipedia.org

WHO, World Health Organization, Antimicrobial resistance, April 2015, © WHO 2015

Wikipedia.org, Ignaz Semmelweis, Wikipedia

# SOURCES

### Kayak (Melting Ice Caps)

Bowermaster, Jon, Global Warming Changing Inuit Lands, Lives, Arctic Expedition Shows, Nationalgegraphic.com, May 15th, 2007, © 1996-2015 National Geographic Society

Brown, Paul, Global warming is killing us too, say Inuit, TheGuardian.com, December 10th 2003, © 2015 Guardian News and Media Limited or its affiliated companies

The Climate Realty Project, climaterealityproject.org

Nasa, National Aeronautics and Space Administration, Climate Kids, "What is global climate change"?, Climatekids.nasa.gov July 2015

Kagan, Mya, What is Global Warming? Whyzz, © Whyzz LLC 2015

NDRC, Natural Resources Defense Council, Global Warming Puts the Arctic on Thin Ice, Nrdc.org, November 2005, © Natural Resources Defense Council

NDRC, Natural Resources Defense Council, The Consequences of Global Warming On Glaciers and Sea Levels, Nrdc.org, November 2005, © Natural Resources Defense Council

### Flashlight (Severe Weather)

Bradford, Alina, Effects of Global Warming, Livescience.com, December 17, 2014, Purch Copyright © 2015

Center for Climate and Energy Solutions, Kids Corner: The Greenhouse Effect and Climate Change, C2es.org

Climate Communication, Overview, Current Extreme Weather & Climate Change, Climatecommunication.org © 2015, Climate Communication

Miller, Peter, What's Causing Extreme Weather?, NationalGeographic.org, August 21, 2012, © 1996-2015 National Geographic Society

### Pearls (Ocean Acidification)

EPA, United States Environmental Protection Agency, Climate Change Indicators in the United States, Epa.gov

IOOS, Integrated Ocean Observing System, Ocean Acidification, National Ocean Service 2014, Ioos.noaa.go

# SOURCES

National Geographic, Ocean Acidification, Carbon Dioxide is Putting Shelled Animals at Risk, Nationalgeographic.com © 1996-2015 National Geographic Society

Kidzworld.com, Ocean Acidification, ©2015 Kidzworld

Wikipedia, Ocean Acidification, Wikipedia.org

## Sweater (Energy Crisis)

Cox, Stan, Cooling a Warming Planet: A Global Air Conditioning Surge, July 10, 2012, Environment 360, e360.yale.edu, © 2008-2015 Yale University

EIA, U.S. Energy Information Administration, How much of world energy consumption and electricity generation is from renewable energy? Eia.gov, December 18, 2014, U.S. Department of Energy

EIA, U.S. Energy Information Administration, Heating and cooling no longer majority of U.S. home energy use, Eia.gov, March 7, 2013, U.S. Department of Energy

eSchoolToday, Renewable Energy, eschooltoday.com, Copyright © 2010 eSchoolToday in association with BusinessGhana.com

eSchoolToday, Non-Renewable Energy, eschooltoday.com, Copyright © 2010 eSchoolToday in association with BusinessGhana.com

Wonderbag, Impact, Wonderbag.com ©2015 Wonderbag Company

## Plastic Bag (Overconsumption)

American Textile Recycling Service, The Circular Economy Explained, Atrscorp.com July 11, 2013

BBC News, Planet Earth's new nemesis? Bbc.co.uk, May 8, 2002, © MMIII

Cole, Cecilia, Overconsumption is costing us the earth and human happiness, TheGuardian.co.uk, June 21, 2010, © 2015 Guardian News and Media Limited or its affiliated companies

Earth Resource Foundation, Campaign Against the Plastic Plague Background Info

Ellen Mac Arthur Foundation, Circular Economy, © Copyright 2015 Ellen Macarthur Foundation

Leonard, Annie, The Story of Stuff, Facts, © 2015 Story of Stuff Project

Wikipedia, Circular Economy. Wikipedia.org

# SOURCES

## Rubber Boots (Overfishing)

Charles Clover, The End of the Line: How Overfishing Is Changing the World and What We Eat

Gibbs, Wayt W., The Plan to Map Illegal Fishing From Space, Wired.com, November 13, 2014, © 2015 Condé Nast

Knowlton, Nancy, Why Do We Have Trouble Talking About Success In Ocean Conservation?, Smithsonian.com , June 12, 2014, © Smithsonian

National Geographic, Overfishing – Plenty of Fish in the Sea? Not Always. NationalGeographic.com, © 1996-2015 National Geographic Society

Leiden, Universiteit, Sustainable approach for the world's fish supply, Sciencedaily.com, January 13, 2015, © 2015 ScienceDaily

Oceana, Wasted Catch: Unsolved Problems in U.S. Fisheries, Oceana.org, March 2014, © 2015 Oceana

Overfishing.org, Overfishing – A Global Disaster, © 2007-2011 Pepijn Koster

## Balloon (Endangered Animals)

Actionbioscience.com, August 2010, © 2000-2015 American Institute of Biological Sciences

Balloonsblow.org

Petersen, Bo, Balloon hazards real or overblown? The Post and Courier, Wildshores. blogspot.hk, January 24, 2011

Kagan, Mya, What does it mean when an animal is endangered, Whyzz.com, © 2015 Whyzz Publications LLC

Mansfield, Kate L., Sea Turtles: Ancient Creatures with Modern Problems, Actionbioscience.com, August 2010, © 2000-2015 American Institute of Biological Sciences

Wildscreen Arkive, Endangered species fact file, Arkive.org © 2015 Wildscreen Arkive, a Wildscreen initiative

Wikipedia, Invasive Species, Wikipedia.org

## Origami (Deforestation)

eSchoolToday, Effects of Deforestation, eschooltoday.com, Copyright © 2010 eSchooltoday in association with BusinessGhana.com

# SOURCES

Kids.Mongabay.com, What is Deforestation, ©2004-2013 mongabay.com

National Geographic, Deforestation, NationalGeographic.org, © 1996-2015 National Geographic Society

National Geographic, Deforestation, NationalGeographic.org, © 1996-2015 National Geographic Society

Wikipedia, Wangari Maathai, Wikipedia.org

WWF, Deforestation, wwf.panda.org © 2015 WWF – World Wide Fund For Nature

## Cook Pot (Energy Poverty)

International Energy Agency, Energy for Cooking in Developing Countries, World Energy Outlook 2006, iea.org, © 2015 OECD/IEA

McFarland, Matt, The Soccer Ball that Helps Kids in Underdeveloped Areas Finish Homework, TheWashingtonPost.com, November 21, 2013, © 2015 Washington Post

Muthiah Radha, Andrés José, Innovation and Investment Needed to Change How the Developing World Cooks, Global Alliance for Clean Cookstoves, Cleancookstoves.org, June 04, 2015, © 2015 United Nations Foundation

Wikipedia, Energy Poverty, Wikipedia.org

## No Idling Sign (Air Pollution)

EDF Environmental Defense Fund, Attention drivers! Turn off your idling engines, edf.org, Copyright © 2015 Environmental Defense Fund

eSchoolToday, Why is Air Pollution such an important issue?, Eschooltoday.com, Copyright © 2010 eSchooltoday in association with BusinessGhana.com

Kagan, Mya, What is pollution, Whyzz.com, © 2015 Whyzz Publications LLC

National Geographic, Air Pollution, NationalGeographic.com, © 1996-2015 National Geographic Society

NRDC, National Resource Defense Council, Ndrc.org

Slanina, Sjaak,The Encyclopedia of Earth, Impacts of air pollution on local to global scale, Eoearth.org, December 21, 2006

WHO, World Health Organization, Burden of disease from ambient and household air pollution, who.int, © WHO 2015

Wikipedia, Air Pollution, Wikipedia.org

# SOURCES

## Flyswatter (Sustainable Agriculture)

Biello, David, Will Organic Food Fail to Feed the World? Scientificamerican.com, April 25, 2012, © 2015 Scientific American, a Division of Nature America, Inc.

Halweil, Brian, Can Organic Farming Feed Us All? World Watch Magazine, May/June 2006, Volume 19, No. 3, © 2013 Worldwatch Institute, worldwatch@worldwatch.org

Grace Communications Foundation, Sustainable Agriculture — The Basics, Sustainabletable.org, © 2015 GRACE Communications Foundation

Lewry Fraser, Insects: the future of food? TheGuardian.com, September 16, 2011, © 2015 Guardian News and Media Limited

Vidal, John, Breed insects to improve human food security: UN report, TheGuardian.com, May13, 2013, © 2015 Guardian News and Media Limited

Wikipedia, Sustainable Agriculture, Wikipedia.org

## Ship (All in One Boat)

[1]Kishore Mahbubani, The Great Convergence, Public Affairs, Perseus Book Company, 2013

[2]Numbers of countries in the world differ: There are 196 countries, the United Nations has 193 members, and the United States officially recognizes 195 countries

Dugal, Bani, Is the nation state past its sell-by-date?, World Economic Forum, Weforum.org, January 22, 2015

Global Kids Connect, What is Global Citizenship, globalkidsconnect.org, ©2004 Global Kids Connect.

Mahbubani, Kishore, Sailing on the Same Boat, Financing for Development, UN.org, June 8, 2015, © 2015 United Nations Department of Economic and Social Affairs

## Stories of Hope

Cooper, Andrea, 8 Amazing Kids Who Make a Difference, Parenting.com, © Copyright 2015, Meredith Corporation.

Guthmann, Edward, Vivienne Harr's lemonade stand story a movie, SFGate.com, January 27, 2014, Hearst Newspapers © Copyright 2015 Hearst Communications, Inc.

# SOURCES

Krochet Kids, About Us, krochetkids.org, © 2015 Krochet Kids Intl.

White, Chelsea, This amazing village in India plants 111 trees every time a girl is born, Globalcitizen.org, May 21, 2015, © 2012-2015 Global Poverty Project, Inc.

## SDGs

The Global Goals, globalgoals.org

United Nations, Open Working Group proposal for Sustainable Development Goals, UN.org, ©Copyright United Nations Department of Economic and Social Affairs

## Glossary

A Student's Guide to Global Climate Change, Greenhouse Gases, EPA.gov, August 28, 2014

Academic Kids, Developing Country, Academickids.com, June 2005

Devlin, Megan, What means citizen, Whyzz.com, © 2015 Whyzz Publications LLC

Dictionary.com, Epidemic, © 2015 Dictionary.com, LLC

Energy Kids, Uranium, U.S. Energy Information Administration, Eia.gov

Gale Encyclopaedia of Medicine, 4th edition, June 10, 2011

HistoryNet, Abolitionist Movement, Historynet.com, © 2015 HistoryNet, LLC

Kagan, Mya, What are bacteria, Whyzz.com, © 2015 Whyzz Publications LLC

Merriam Webster Dictionary, Atrocity, Merriam-webster.com, © 2015 Merriam-Webster, Incorporated

Kids.Net.Au, NATO, Encyclopedia.kids.net.au, © 2015 Kids.Net.Au

Niedermaier, Constanze, 33 Things to Explain the World to Kids, Ecosystem, © 2015 Whyzz Publications LLC

Merriam Webster Dictionary, Sustainable, Merriam-webster.com, © 2015 Merriam-Webster, Incorporated

Swabey, Peter, The Hyperconnected Economy, Economyinsights.com, October 10, 2014, Copyright © The Economist Newspaper Limited 2015

Wikipedia, Animal Welfare, Wikipedia.org

# DON'T MISS:

"33 Things to Explain the World" offers conversation starters for fun and meaningful family time. Familiar, everyday objects help parents discuss topics like Atmosphere (Apple Peel), Biodiversity (Honey), Agriculture (Perfume), Art (Urinal), Moral Values (Mirror) or Dignity (Camera).

The goal of the book is to show children how everything in the world has relevance for them and how everything is interrelated.

## Available on Amazon.com